Successful Consulting

Successful Consulting

Mastering the Five Challenges that can Make or Break you as an Independent Consultant

- The *Readiness* Challenge
- The *Financial Reality* Challenge
- The *Marketing and Business Development* Challenge
- The *Communicating* Challenge
- The *Client Relationship* Challenge

PLUS

21 Practical and Proven Tools that Every Consultant Needs to be Successful

Fred and Peggy Fisher

iUniverse, Inc.

New York Lincoln Shanghai

Successful Consulting
Mastering the Five Challenges that can Make
or Break you as an Independent Consultant

iUniverse books may be ordered through booksellers or by contacting:

iUniverse
2021 Pine Lake Road, Suite 100
Lincoln, NE 68512
www.iuniverse.com
1-800-Authors (1-800-288-4677)

ISBN-13: 978-0-595-36479-4 (pbk)
ISBN-13: 978-0-595-80912-7 (ebk)
ISBN-10: 0-595-36479-9 (pbk)
ISBN-10: 0-595-80912-X (ebk)

Printed in the United States of America

Contents

If you think you can, you can.
And if you think you can't, you're right.

Mary Kay Ash

A Perspective on Consulting from the Trenches

When we came back in 1987 from a four-and-one-half year assignment in Africa, we learned that the university where Fred had taught for eleven years had eliminated his department and "position." As part of the over fifty gang, and out of touch after nearly a half decade "on the road," our options for earning a living in the safe lane were few. Consulting looked like a reasonable option. When all else fails, become a consultant. How we got to that decision may be instructive for many of you who *wannabe* consultants. For those who still are struggling to be more successful as consultants, our tale will no doubt be familiar.

Like most consultants, our careers were not shaped to point us in this vocational direction. Fred had been a city manager and a few other associated things in his pre-academic life. Peggy started her career as a nurse and put that on hold to become a full-time mother. Neither of us felt inclined to return to endeavors of the past. For Fred, trying to relocate with another institution of higher learning was also out of the question. He had been one of those rebels who thought that academic tenure was an arcane system to reward the incompetent. Consequently, he eked out a living in academia by stringing together six and twelve month contracts on emerging and fading targets of opportunity— hardly the stuff to beef up a curriculum vitae.

Peggy on the other hand had morphed from the pre-family stage of her nursing career to managing a national professional/educational institution. The opportunity for Fred to take a long term contract in Africa to work with low-income housing projects, and to take the contract through the university, was too much intermediate security to pass up. Peggy resigned reluctantly to keep the family together, and we went off to Nairobi, Kenya, to save the world. Although Fred was still on the university's payroll, he was also conveniently out of sight, out of mind, and subsequently out of a job when we returned from the "Dark Continent." So much for career and life planning!

As reality seeped into our collective cranium, we realized our earning-a-livelihood options were not plentiful. And then, the creative juices flowed, the lights started flashing, and we heard ourselves exclaiming to each other, "We could become consultants!" After all, we understood international development funding peculiarities—and, in a pique of typical American arrogance, convinced ourselves that the downtrodden and unfortunate of the world needed us out there. Peggy had also used her inventive skills to land a full-time job in Kenya, so we were ready! Since we had a few personal contacts in international agencies and the beltway vultures that hover over them, we began to cash in these chips. Most of those we consulted were reasonably optimistic on our behalf, an attitude that is easy to assume when it's not your neck that's on the line.

As a university professor, Fred had done his share of consulting to supplement the family income, but this was going to be a full-time commitment: no benefits, no steady income, and no security blanket to hunker under. It was scary. Peggy wasn't keen on jetting around the world at the drop of a short-term contract, so we carved out a stay-at-home, non-paying role for her as business manager. This meant that Fred could work non-stop while she paid the bills, collected the fees, and fielded queries about his availability.

For openers, it meant cutting our on-going expenses to the bone. We bought an old farmhouse in rural Pennsylvania, heeding the advice of others that we needed to be close enough to Washington to commute if necessary. From our perspective, we wanted to be far enough away to escape the rising costs and hectic pace associated with metropolitan living as well as closer to the kind of rural life-style we had experienced in our youth. But, the bottom line in this decision was **the bottom line.** With no steady income, we needed to hunker down.

The first year or so was lean, as it is for most new consultants, and the next few years—downright mean. Peddling one's ass-ets a day at a time is hard, demanding work and downright lonely if you decide to carve out the world as your territory. In one three month stretch of short contracts, Fred circled the globe twice, one eastward and the other to the west. His assignments had him working on three continents during each of these long-distance treks with only three days back home between them. Just enough time to do the laundry and experience the ire of a lonely and frustrated spouse who was staffing our international headquarters, which was and continues to be located in the back of our one-car garage. The irony of this strung-out lifestyle didn't escape either of us over the years. Peggy was, for the most part, tied to the office lining up other contracts so she could be even more miffed about Fred being gone.

The bottom line—we survived. We earned a decent living—decent, that is, by Upper Adams County standards. Like most free-lance consultants, we remind ourselves during our morning ablutions in some God forsaken place that money isn't everything. Do we regret the last seventeen years of craziness? No. Would we do it over again even if we would have had other options at the time we started? Yes. We also think we have learned a few things that might help other wannabe and struggling consultants as they head down a similar trail.

Lessons learned from the trenches

Here are a few of the broad-brush details on how we found relative success as free-lance consultants.

- We carved out a niche market based on our previous experiences and expertise. For us it was capacity and institution building support with local governments and non-governmental organizations (NGOs). While it helps to narrow your focus and define your market, it is imperative to have sound experience and a definable expertise if you want to be successful as a free-lance consultant. Otherwise, your potential clients might as well hire their relatives. This happens on occasion but don't take it personally.

- We've been willing to take on all kinds of assignments in all kinds of places as long as we felt competent to serve the client's needs and the assignment didn't contradict our values. In other words, we haven't been particularly fussy.

- We've never hired others on a permanent basis even though some projects required the efforts of many. When we needed help to carry out a project, we hired individuals on short-term, project-specific contracts. For example, in order to conduct a complicated management assessment project in Bangladesh, we hired twenty-five local specialists on individual contracts.

We did not want the responsibility of finding work to keep others gainfully employed.

- We decided early on in our consulting career that we would rather spend our time working with clients than hustling their business. Hopefully, we can help you make sense out of this non sequitur. Every day spent on marketing translates into an increase in your daily fee, if you want to achieve your financial goals as a consultant. By working at a much lower daily rate than your comparable colleagues are charging is a rather weird and twisted marketing strategy, but it works. It's a matter of deciding how you want to spend your time—consulting or marketing. Of course, if you adopt this strategy, you may need to come to grips with your ego. Just because your daily rate is lower than your competition doesn't mean you're worth less per day—just getting paid less. Unfortunately, this strategy hinges on establishing a client baseline you can depend on. We'll have more to say about this in the sections on the *financing* and *marketing challenges.*

- We have rarely charged overhead on our time and expenses. As a result, we have forced ourselves to keep overhead costs to a minimum. We think this benefits the client. It also simplifies our billing arrangements and helps secure longer term client relationships. It depends on how you want to spend your time as a free-lance consultant and how much you think you're worth per day.

These are some of the consulting challenges we deal with in this Guide. Free-lance consulting is a tough business. It can grind you down. On the other hand, it can be exhilarating. To help you make a decision to become a full-time free-lance consultant, or to improve your lot as a current free-lancer in this business, we will focus on five challenges that are central to becoming and remaining a successful consultant.

But, be forewarned! You will encounter a few contradictions between what we suggest you might do to be successful as a consultant—and what we personally have done as independent consultants. For example, we never did figure out how to bill clients what we are worth. Of course, what we thought we were worth at any given time was often in stark contrast with what our clients had in mind. The *billable conundrum* discussed in the section on Financial Reality is still on our "to-do" list.

The third edition of *The New Dictionary of Cultural Literacy* gives credit to Plato for coining the phrase "necessity is the mother of invention." It's a metaphor for describing how a need or problem encourages creative efforts to meet the need or solve the problem. Successful consulting, as we are suggesting, is also the mother of invention. We hope you find our twenty-first century version of professional motherhood useful as you strive for success as a full-time, free-lance consultant.

What to Expect from This Guide

This Guide deals with five basic challenges that can make or break you as an independent consultant: *Readiness*; *Financial Reality*; *Marketing and Business Development*; *Communicating*; and the *Consultant-Client Relationship*. The final section deals with a few *Basic Survival Tools* that we have either discovered or developed over the years and which have helped us keep reasonably sane and solvent.

The professional landscape is littered with consultants who didn't quite make it in this quirky business. The *Readiness* challenge deals with some of the basics of consulting. What does it mean to be a consultant? What kind of consultant do you want to be? Or, if you are already a full-time consultant and struggling, how ready are you to make decisions that will help you either be successful or get out of the business before it pulls you down? Can you manage your time? If not, can you learn this ancient art of survival? If you haven't already taken a successful consultant to lunch to figure out how she does it, do it!

The *Financial Reality* challenge covers such things as how to construct a personal budget (what is needed to continue your current lifestyle?) while simultaneously assembling a business budget. In addition, we will look at the hard cold facts of generating enough revenue to keep the wolves from the door—or at least the loan sharks; setting your professional fees; developing a business plan; and, most importantly, coping with billing-rate depression.

The *Marketing and Business Development* challenge deals with some key survival skills: determining the market needs for your services; the importance of relationships and how to maintain them; the difference between direct and indirect marketing and the pros and cons of each; building and sustaining client relationships; and the scourge of proposal writing and RFP-chasing. RFP? That's the ubiquitous *requests-for-proposal* charade that government agencies operate to drive consultants crazy, bankrupt, or both.

The *Communicating* challenge focuses on such skills as documentation; making presentations; the fine arts of listening and asking questions; giving feedback (i.e., telling your client what she already knows but doesn't want to hear); and other good mouth and ear stuff that can make or break your consulting career.

The *Client Relations* challenge, of course, includes all the above and more. It provides such helpful hints as how to establish a psychological and working contract with your client; how to deal with resistance; the fine art of collaboration; and how to say goodbye at the completion of one consulting assignment so it doesn't close the door to future opportunities.

Finally, we have included a few consulting tools for your consideration. They are based in large measure on the authors' biases about what is needed and what works in most consulting situations. They are merely a sample of the more complete toolkit you will assemble over time as you become successful in this business. This final section we have labeled *A Few Basic Tools to Add to Your Survival Kit*. It includes:

- Some thoughts on time management. If you don't manage your time, it will eat you alive!

- How to establish a psychological contract with your client. Sounds like psycho-babble, but this professional mating dance can determine the fate of your consultancy.

- Closely aligned with the contracting phase is the fine art of dealing with resistance.

- Action research has been around for a long time. Nevertheless, the basics of this process are fundamental to consultant-client interaction. We've wrapped it around something we call participative decision making and problem solving.

- Information and data collection tactics are key to action research so we will spend more time outlining the various ways to add knowledge legitimacy to your consulting ventures.

- A bread and butter skill: facilitating visioning and strategic planning sessions.

- Some thoughts on staff development and training interventions as consulting staples.

- A reminder of the importance of interpersonal communication skills to surviving with class.

We hope that you will expand on these tools as you build your consulting business. One way to be financially successful as a consultant is to develop an increasingly wide range of analytical and interpersonal methods, tools, practices, and experiences that can be replicated without starting from ground zero. For example, you might develop a basic communication course for employees who staff reception desks based on work with a new hotel that is opening in your community. With some fine tuning you could use the same materials to train the employees of a local government that has just initiated a one-stop center for processing various kinds of permits and licenses. The key phrase in this example is *fine tuning.* It is important to tailor each intervention based on the client's needs.

As you move on to the discussions about the five key challenges of building and sustaining a successful consulting business, you will discover that we have quoted some authors who have made major contributions to management in general and consulting in particular. We encourage you to build a reference library of books like the ones we have quoted from in this guide. Our success as consultants is due in large part to the mentors with whom we have met along the way. Some, like Neely Gardner, Frank Sherwood, Charlie Seashore, Jim Pritchard, Ana Vasilache, and David Tees, we have worked with directly. Others, like Kurt Lewin, we have met only through their writings. Nevertheless, they have contributed to our understanding of this profession and are much more than just endnotes on the last page of this Guide. Their nurturing and support continues even as we write these words of appreciation. Finally, our appreciation for the expert editing efforts of Allison Singley.

It's time to take the Challenge. Are you ready?

If it be now, 'tis not to come;
If it be not to come, it will be now;
If it be not now, yet it will come;
The readiness is all.

William Shakespeare: *Hamlet*

I. The *Readiness* Challenge

What you can expect to find in this chapter:

- Common consulting terminology: *getting with the lingo*
- What consultants do for a living
- A look at some operating options
- A systems perspective to the consulting process
- The need for self reflection and assessment before taking the plunge
- The *Moment of Truth* Inquiry: Parts One and Two
- The importance of lunching with a successful consultant
- So, you decided to become a consultant—what next?

In order to get the optimum benefit from this Guide, it will be helpful to understand some of the common terms that are used in the consulting business. It will also keep us operating on the same page as we work our way through the various challenges that most consultants face early in their careers.

- **Consultant:** Someone who is in the position to have some influence over an individual, group, organization, or community but has no direct authority to make changes or to implement them. In other words, speak with authority but don't exercise it!

- **Consulting:** The application of knowledge, skills, experience, and other relevant attributes within a client setting to help the client bring about improvements. The longer you consult, the greater should be the accumulation of these wide-ranging attributes—and the more valuable your contribution to the client's well-being.

- **Client:** A person, work group, organization, or community that engages the services of a consultant to achieve certain results.

- **Intervention:** Any action a consultant takes in collaboration with a client resulting in changes in individual, group, organization, or community performance.

- **Facilitating:** A guided process of helping individuals, groups, organizations, or communities become more efficient and effective in their interactions with others.

- **Contracting:** The process of reaching a mutual agreement between the client and the consultant about the purpose of the consultation, the roles and responsibilities of each party, their wants and needs in the working relationship, and the nature of the intended results.

While these definitions are intended to apply to most consulting situations, it is helpful to understand that consulting is often described in professional literature as either *expert* or *process* consulting.

- **Expert consulting** is often described as either *the purchase of expertise,* resulting from the client defining the need and concluding she has neither the expertise or the time to fulfill the need, or the *doctor-patient* relationship based on a diagnosis that results in the consultant prescribing the actions (cures) to be taken by the client.

- **Process consulting** is a collaborative process between the consultant and client involving diagnosis, decision-making, problem solving, and internal capacity building designed to make the client more self-reliant in similar situations in the future.

This Guide is based largely on the *process consulting* approach although many of the concepts, principles, and strategies covered in the Guide can be applied to both approaches.

Before we move on, we want to comment briefly on the categories of clients mentioned above. While many of you may choose to focus on groups, teams, or organizations as your primary clientele, it is helpful to think about individuals and communities as important clients as well. Often, individual leaders can benefit from your interventions in one-to-one dialogue sessions. And, larger communities encompassing various groups and organizations can make for exciting clients. In other words, don't limit your ideas about what the term *client* means.

Definitions are fine but there is more you need to know about consultants and consulting if you want to be successful

Consultants by any other name: Just who are we? Consultants are usually individuals who are hired for short periods of time to help organizations, teams, or even individuals perform tasks they are not able to perform themselves or through the efforts of their members or employees. Consultants are usually categorized as external or internal consultants and as technical or process consultants.

The role of *internal consultant* is a more recent management strategy employed in large organizations. Internal consultants are often members of an internal staff group responsible for providing organization-wide functions like human resources, finance, or information technology. They "consult" with operating agencies within the larger organization to help them carry out specific organization-wide, staff-related functions. For example, a large corporation might decide to employ internal consultants to help operating departments install ISO standards and systems to insure their compliance.

External consultants are individuals who consult with other individuals, groups or teams of individuals, organizations, or groups of organizations on an "as-needed" basis through some type of contractual arrangement. As an external consultant, you have many choices in terms of your employment. You can work alone, in collaboration with other consultants, or as an employee of a consulting organization. You can work part-time or full-time; either as a technical or process consultant; or utilizing a combination of these options.

While all these options are fine, this Guide is targeted to those of you who decide to:

1) work as an individual consultant full-time;

2) create a loose consortium of individual consultants who collaborate when it is advantageous to one or more of them in maintaining their own individual businesses; or,

3) establish a consulting firm including two or more full-time consultants.

Based on which of these options you decide to pursue in your career as a full-time consultant, some of the responses to the various challenges we will be discussing will need to be modified to accommodate your decision. For example, the decisions and costs involved in establishing an individual consulting business could differ substantially from those necessary to establish a consulting firm with two or more full-time consultants.

What do consultants do? As mentioned in the definitions, consulting is most often divided into two general categories, *technical* and *process* consulting, although they are not exclusive. Some consultants offer both kinds of consulting services.

- *Technical consultants* bring to the client an expertise the client either doesn't have within their organization or may require on a short-term basis to supplement the capacity of full-time internal staff members, based on a specific need. Most technical consultants are associated with a specific discipline like engineering, or information systems, or financial or general management. As a technical consultant, you need both expertise and experience to be considered legitimate by your perspective clients. You may also be asked to perform a wide range of services, from diagnosing needs and planning operational changes to installing new operating systems and evaluating on-going programs and services. In other words, you are hired for your technical expertise.

- *Process consultants* focus on collaborative diagnosis and problem solving with the explicit goal of passing on to the client their diagnostic and problem solving skills. In other words, most process consultants consider themselves as cloning specialists. As a process consultant, you give equal attention to the tasks involved in addressing technical issues and the human interactions that take place in the process. As Peter Block, author of *Flawless Consulting*, says, "When consultants work through a collaborative role, they don't solve problems for managers, they apply their special skills to help managers solve problems." (1981, p.22) Process consultation often involves a wide range of skills, including coaching, training, group process facilitating, and something called action research.

What are your operating options as a consultant? Theoretically and operationally, you have many options to consider in conducting your consulting business. You can operate as an individual full-time or part-time entrepreneur. You can be a member of a coalition of individual consultants who collaborate when it meets their needs or interests. Or, you can be a part of a larger consulting firm. If you are successful, you can develop a consulting firm where your employees do all the work while you spend your time at the beach. Each option has its benefits and its costs. All options require that you keep your cell phone handy and turned on.

As a consultant, who are your potential clients? Fortunately, we can work at any level of society. We can consult with individuals, task-oriented work groups, technical and management teams, organizations, communities, and inter-organizational consortiums. It is not uncommon for consultants to work with a rich mix of clientele. Consultants who suffer from boredom need to get with the program and expand their client options!

How and why do individuals like you become consultants? First of all, it is important to have educational credentials and practical experience in the discipline for which you decide to become a consultant. Otherwise, you will have a difficult time marketing your expertise. And, you may have a legitimacy problem as well. Or, you might see an opportunity to work as a consultant in a related field of endeavor and take a chance that it will lead to a new career. For example, you might be working in the public relations department of a large corporation and decide to chuck it all to free-lance as a PR specialist, working with community-based organizations.

The best answers to *why* and *how* individuals decide to become full-time consultants are within each prospective consultant. In other words: Why do *you* want to be a consultant? What do *you* have to offer prospective clients as a consultant?

Consulting Options and the Big Picture

Let's assume you want to be a full-time consultant and operate a consulting business of your own. As an independent consultant, you have several options.

Option One: Concentrate on a major personal skill and competency—one you can exploit to serve prospective clients. For example, you might be good at conducting strategic planning activities, or helping organizations install performance measurement systems, or providing mediation services. This approach usually means having many different clients and shorter consulting assignments. It is an approach you can use to get started, but don't plan to build a lifelong career around it. Use it to broaden your skills and expand your client contacts.

Option Two: Concentrate on a specific discipline, like financial management, or a client group, like small businesses, local governments, or non-governmental organizations. This option narrows the potential client targets of opportunity but allows you to become recognized as an expert within a defined area of consultation.

Option Three: Become a consulting generalist, building your expertise as a process consultant and capacity builder. This presumes a consulting approach that involves collaboration with the client on all phases of the intervention. This option often results in longer term relationships with specific clients and opportunities to work with a variety of staff and line functions within their organizations.

The Bigger Picture: Regardless of the option you think you want to pursue early in your new career as a consultant, it is important to understand and appreciate the larger framework within which consultancies can and should take place. By understanding consulting as a process, rather than a quick fix of the client's most urgent problem, you not only help the client resolve the problem by digging deeper to the root causes, you also build your consulting business.

For example, many consulting assignments are confined to carrying out a specific assignment with a client. You are called in to perform a specific task:

- To help a small business management team prepare a strategic plan.

- To work with a group of line supervisors to instruct them on how to develop financial performance measures for their work unit.

- To conduct a skill-building workshop for local government budget officers on how to hold neighborhood meetings in conjunction with preparing the annual budget.

In each of these consulting assignments is an opportunity to help the organization bring about a more comprehensive and longer term series of changes.

- The strategic planning assignment could provide an opportunity to work with departments in carrying out new programs or services resulting from the planning process.

- In the second example, the consultant might help line supervisors develop programs for actually implementing performance measures working with their employees. Learning how to develop performance measures is very different from implementing them.

- In the final option, the consultant might help local governments develop monitoring systems to track the results of participatory budgeting processes. This could be followed by further consulting assistance to establish neighborhood service units based on citizen feedback. This assumes you see local governments as a viable clientele group to exploit in your consulting initiatives.

The consultant, in each of these examples, has helped the client generate a value-added dimension to the initial consulting assignment. The consultant has also generated new business. Seeing how each consulting assignment fits into the client's overall policy, planning, and operating frameworks is one of the best ways to market consulting services. But, it also requires the consultant to develop a more sophisticated understanding of the consultant-client relationship.

Each consulting assignment represents a dynamic process between the consultant and the client that has the potential to benefit both parties through future interventions. This longer-range, comprehensive approach to building a consulting business can be described as a series of activities. There are certain stages in the process that are important to each assignment, even the short ones, and these stages need to be honored. In more complex and comprehensive assignments, the process involves all the stages. In their totality, they represent a process for bringing about planned changes within complex settings like organizations and communities.

British consultant Mick Cope provides an in-depth look at consulting as a dynamic process between consultants and clients in his insightful book, *The Seven Cs of Consulting*. His seven stages provide a framework for understanding consulting as a major intervention strategy for bringing about changes in complex organizations and social settings. His treatment of the stages of the consulting process is among the best available anywhere. We encourage those who want to better understand the holistic nature of this business to read Cope's book.

> Every good consultant needs to develop a reference library. From time to time We will be referring to other authors whom we believe have made significant contributions to consulting and the processes that successful consultants use in their daily work. Think about adding these authors to your team of silent and reflective advisors.

The seven stages, according to Cope, are:

1. **Client:** Define the client's orientation of the world, their perception of the situation, what goals they have regarding the final outcome, and who has power to influence the outcome. Reach a clear agreement as to what value you will deliver to the client and what value they will offer in return. The essence of this stage is to understand the client and the problem.

2. **Clarity:** Determine the nature and detail of the problem to be addressed. Identify what and who is to be included and excluded from the change and determine what areas pose a risk for the assignment. The primary question to understand is, "What is going on?"

3. **Create:** Use creative techniques to develop a sustainable solution. Critically develop a solution that is measured against clear success criteria, take as divergent a view as possible to find potential options, and then choose the option that meets the defined criteria.

4. **Change:** Understand the fundamental aspects that are driving the change process and, in particular, the human factors that need to be managed.

5. **Confirm**: Ensure that change has taken place, using quantitative and qualitative measures.

6. **Continue**: Ensure that the change can and will be sustained. Use learning that emerges from the transition and change agent skills to foster the sharing and use of new knowledge and skills.

7. **Close**: End the engagement with the client, emphasizing the need to understand the final outcomes, the added value, new learning, and what further action you might undertake. (2003, p. 9)

Cope sees the consulting process from the perspective of planned change and the importance of engaging the client actively in each of the seven stages in his consulting framework. Nevertheless, he also reminds us that each stage in the process can stand alone or run parallel to others.

His consulting model is similar to other managing change processes dating back to the work of Kurt Lewin and his colleagues nearly a half century ago. Lewin's action research model, as modified by others who followed in his footsteps, includes the following steps:

1. Initial contact and reconnaissance of the situation;

2. Building a collaborative, problem solving relationship among the key stakeholders, i.e., consultant and client;

3. Problem finding and analysis;

4. Planning a course of action;

5. Organization and resource mobilization;

6. Implementation of the desired course of action(s), and

7. Impact evaluation.

These comprehensive models of consulting can help you think about and plan for consulting assignments that will engage the client in a longer-term change process. While most consultations will be much more confined, it is important to understand and appreciate the more comprehensive context within which consultants can operate.

From the perspective of managing a consulting business, it is often easier to get more work from a current client than to seek out new ones.

Before you hang up your CONSULTANT FOR HIRE sign, engage in some serious self-assessment and reflection

Your success as a consultant will depend on many things: your educational and work background, experience, personal traits, contacts, willingness to take risks, financial requirements, and a number of other variables. Before you take any concrete steps to establish a consulting business:

- Ask yourself some tough task-oriented questions concerning the reality of establishing a new profession and business.

- Take stock of your personal strengths and possible deficiencies as they relate to these realities.

- Remind yourself that you are about to start down a path that can be fraught with considerable uncertainty, ambiguity, and moments of economic-driven panic.

To help in getting answers to these challenging tasks, take a few moments and complete the following *Moment of Truth* dialogue with the rational part of your brain. Depending on what you find out about yourself, you may save the time of reading the rest of this Guide.

The *Moment of Truth* Inquiry: Part One

1. What will be your consulting focus, e.g., financial management, general management, public relations, conflict resolution, executive development, how to survive as a consultant, (you name it!)? The clearer you can be about who you want to be as a consultant, and what your specialization will be, the better your chances of success. You need to **FOCUS**! If you can't, you may want to consider checking out the *Help Wanted* ads in your local paper. So FOCUS!

2. Who will be your primary clients? Small businesses, corpora-
    tions, local governments, non-governmental organizations,
    professionals such as financial managers, executives who need
    counseling in ethics? You need to be able to identify who your
    primary clients will be. If not, well…the *Help Wanted* ads are
    always an option. So, one more time: **FOCUS!**

3. Based on this gut-wrenching experience, just what special
    knowledge and skills do you think you have to offer as a
    consultant that these clients will be willing to spend their hard-
    earned money on? Yes, it's time to be specific!

4. How much work experience do you have in the consulting
    field on which you plan to focus? *Winging it* may get you in the
    door, but sticking around to be helpful to your clients takes a
    solid track record of experience. Take a few moments and list
    these work experiences before your client asks for them.

5. How confident are you that your knowledge, skills, and experi-
    ence are marketable in the discipline, and the clientele areas, in
    which you plan to provide consulting services?

    Very confident? _____
    Somewhat confident? _____
    Not very confident? _____

If you aren't fully confident about your ability to sell yourself and
your experience and qualifications, you may want to reconsider your
decision to become a consultant at this time in your life and professional career.

Assuming you made it this far in your journey of self inquiry, there
is one more burning question that you and those who depend on you
for financial support **must** ask.

6. How prepared are you to live with the financial consequences
    of starting a new business and operating without a steady and
    reliable income?

    Very: ___
    Somewhat: ___
    Haven't thought about it: ___

And, what about those who depend upon your financial support for their well-being?

7. _____

(You are encouraged to add other questions to this personal inquisition.)

If you made it this far, it's time to check out your consulting aptitude

The *Moment of Truth* Inquiry: Part Two

The following are some generally recognized personal qualities that will determine your success as a consultant. Rate each of these qualities using the following three point scale: 1=not at all; 2=somewhat; 3=yes!

1. Are you self-motivated? [ ]

2. Are you a hard worker? [ ]

3. Can you get along with many kinds of people? [ ]

4. Are you an excellent communicator? [ ]

5. Do you like writing proposals and reports? [ ]

6. Are you a risk taker? [ ]

7. Are you a good problem solver? [ ]

8. Are you a person who can see "the big picture"? [ ]

9. And yet, someone who can also pay attention to details? [ ]

10. Are you known for your objectivity? [ ]

11. Are you ambitious? [ ]

12. Are you self-confident? [ ]

13. Are you creative? [ ]

14. Are you healthy? (Consulting can be a grueling business.) [ ]

15. Do you like to market and sell yourself and your ideas? [ ]

16. Are you known by others as having good judgment? [ ]

17. Can you set personal goals and follow them to completion? [ ]

18. Do you adapt easily to new situations? [ ]

19. Do you like to work with people? [ ]

20. Are you trustworthy? [ ]

21. Can you tolerate ambiguity? [ ]

22. Are you flexible? [ ]

23. Do you have good analytical skills? [ ]

24. Are you self-disciplined? [ ]

25. Are you prepared to live with the uncertainty of not having a regular paycheck?[ ]

Add up your scores. If you were honest with yourself and scored more than 60 points, you will probably be successful as a consultant. If you scored between 40 and 60, you probably have the potential to be a successful consultant. Nevertheless, you will need to work on those qualities you scored the lowest. If you scored under 40 points, you should probably think about another profession.

Take a Successful Consultant to Lunch

Another insightful book on consulting is *The Consultant's Quick Start Guide to Consulting* by Elaine Biech. She suggests you take a consultant to lunch and subject that person to a friendly inquisition—before you make your final decision to become a full-time consultant. For this privilege, she suggests that you also pay for her lunch. Like any competent consultant would, we have taken her good idea and transformed it into our own set of culinary-oriented inquiries. Nevertheless, you might want to check out her ideas as well. (2001, p.18)

- What are the most important factors that have contributed to your success as a consultant?

- Why? *(By the way, this is the most important word in the consulting language.)*

- What motivated you to become a consultant?

- How did you decide what kind of consultant you wanted to be?

- Has that focus changed over time, and why?

- Could you describe what the first year or so was like in starting and building your consulting business?

- What's the basic operating structure of your business, and why did you decide to operate this way?

- How did you decide what kinds of clients you wanted to work with initially?

- Have you been able to concentrate on this client base or has it changed over the years?

- What does a typical month in your life as a consultant look like? In other words, how do you spend your time in being a successful consultant?

- How important is marketing and how do you go about it?

- If you had to focus on only one marketing strategy, what would it be?

- What do you like best about being a consultant?

- And, least?

- If you could start over again as a consultant, what would you do differently?

- If you were on my side of this conversation, what other questions would you ask?

- (Add a few more questions of your own over dessert.)

Spend some time thinking about what you learned and how you might use this information to make your decision about becoming a consultant. Then sit down with a good friend and talk about what you learned. Ask your friend to rephrase the relevant questions and ask them of you using a future timeframe context. For example, *what marketing activities do you plan to conduct if you decide to become a consultant?*

Assuming You Decide to Become a Full-Time Consultant, What Are the Next Steps?

Before you make that final decision to become a full-time consultant, it will be important to carry out the following three steps. The first is to determine what kind of consulting you want to offer, based on your knowledge, skills, experience, and personal qualities.The second is to gain some assurance that there is a clientele system that can sustain your consulting aspirations. The third is to conduct a detailed reality check on what is involved financially in establishing a full-time consulting business. Here is a detailed look at these three important tasks.

Step 1: Define who you want to be as a consultant: Assuming you are serious about becoming a consultant, return to the *Moment of Truth* Inquiry questionnaires you completed earlier and review your answers based on the additional information you now have about consulting. Update your answers to the key decision questions in Part I of this exercise in reality. Also, review your answers to the consulting aptitude questionnaire. If you gave yourself scores of 1 or 2 on any of the questions, think about the potential negative consequences of these personal characteristics when you begin your full-time work as a consultant. Secondly, jot down some specific steps you might take to overcome or minimize them.

This becomes your first professional development plan to work on as you begin your new profession. If you didn't complete these tasks, we strongly recommend that you do. If you can't define who you want to be as a consultant and if you can't assess your relative strengths and areas of needed improvement in relation to the kind of consultant you want to be, you are probably off to a weak start.

Step 2: Conduct a client reality check: Before you develop a business plan, to be discussed next, it will be important to conduct an informal survey of your prospective clients. Here are a few thoughts on how to undertake this task.

Start with the organizations you already are working with in one way or another.

- Explore with these organizations how your knowledge, skills, and experience might fit into various levels of each organization, based on a consulting arrangement.

- Never close any discussion with a prospective client without asking, "Whom else do you know who might need my services, or at least might be willing to hear about my new consulting business?"

- Based on the type of client individuals, groups, organizations, or communities you plan to work with, make a map of their spheres of influence or engagement. For example, they may be associated with professional associations, educational institutions, foundations, NGOs, or specific kinds of funding agencies. In theory, they may become part of your future client base, or they might be potential sources of funding for projects with the client base you plan to target for your services.

- Contact consulting firms that might be interested in hiring you on an as-needed basis, when they need extra help.

- Contact local educational institutions. Many consultants teach part-time, not just to supplement their income but to expand their contacts and increase their credibility with operating clients.

- Attend professional association conferences or trade shows to talk to delegates about your new business venture and the services you will be providing.

- Add to this list all the potential contacts you think can give you a more realistic estimate of your initial level of success as a consultant. These initial contacts and discussions are also a subtle way to start your promotion and advertising campaign.

Are You Ready?

If you've taken the *Readiness Challenge* seriously, you should be ready either to move on to the next stage of this self-inquisition process or to put this slightly used document up for re-sale on e-bay. Assuming you are still confident there is a consultant lurking in your bathroom mirror, move on to the next stage which deals with the financial realities of consulting.

*It's not that money makes everything good; it's
that no money makes everything bad.*

Yiddish proverb

II. The *Financial Reality* Challenge

What you can expect to find in this chapter:

- How to determine the costs of your first year of full-time consulting
- The need for fixed assets: the consultant's starter kit
- The short and long term realities of generating a sustainable cash flow
- Billing options
- The billable days nightmare and how to cope with it
- The need for specialized help in growing the business

The financial realities of being a consultant are both easy and complex: easy because you will know before too long whether your talents will keep you solvent and complex because the financial realities will drive many more of your personal and professional decisions than you ever imagined possible. To help you sort through this monetary thicket, we will look at the tasks of putting together personal and business budgets, the need for fixed assets, revenue realities and options, the usefulness of a business plan, and the need for specialized help from time to time. When you combine each of these components, they represent the financial reality check of engaging in full-time consultancy work.

This reality check is based on several important assumptions.

1. You plan to become a full-time consultant.

2. Consulting fees will be your primary source of income.

3. You plan to establish your full-time consulting business at a specific time in the near future. This final assumption may sound a bit strange, but it is needed in order to put together a realistic budget for your first full year of consulting.

You may need to modify these assumptions later on, based on this reality check. But first it is important to determine what your expenses will be for the first year of your new business and how much you will need to charge for your services in order to balance your budget. The following exercises are designed to help you understand the fiscal realities of becoming a full-time consultant before you make the decision to do so.

Expenditure estimates for the initial year of full-time consulting

Part One: A projection of current living costs

Given these assumptions, put together a financial budget for the first twelve months of your new business. Base these estimates on your most recent twelve months of income and expenditures. Here are some general ideas about what categories to include. You may need to alter the individual categories to relate to your own experience. Start with your current expenditures and project what you believe they will be in the first year of your full-time consulting business.

EXPENDITURES:	Current year:	First year operating estimates:
Housing: Mortgage payment/rent:	_____	_____
Utilities:		
Electricity:	_____	_____
Telephone:	_____	_____
Others, if any:	_____	_____
Food:	_____	_____
Clothing:	_____	_____
Transportation:		
Automobile related expenses:		
Loan payments:	_____	_____
Repairs/maintenance:	_____	_____
Fuel:	_____	_____
Insurance:	_____	_____
Mass transportation:	_____	_____
Medical: Insurance premiums:	_____	_____
Other medical costs:	_____	_____

(Are these medical expenses currently paid, in part or in full, by your employer? If so, how will they change?)

Other insurance:	_____	_____
School expenses, if any:	_____	_____
Child care, if relevant:	_____	_____
Entertainment (may go up!):	_____	_____
Professional development, books, etc.:	_____	_____
Taxes: List by type and amount:		
_____	_____	_____
_____	_____	_____
Interest: credit cards, loans, etc.:	_____	_____
Charitable contributions:	_____	_____
Major purchases:	_____	_____

(See following worksheet for a list of possible equipment and other one-time costs you might need to incur in your first year of operation as a consultant.)

Others:		
_____	_____	_____
_____	_____	_____
Yearly totals:	_____	_____

INCOME:	**Current year:**	**First year estimates:**
Salary and wages:	_____	_____

(Base your estimated income for the first year of consulting on the fees you believe you will be able to generate as a full-time consultant.)

Other income:	_____	_____
Yearly totals:	_____	_____

Assuming you will not be able to reach your full potential income in the initial year of operation, determine the shortfall between income and expenditures. Also assume that this shortfall will need to be covered by savings or other means.

Shortfall to be covered by other than consulting fees during the initial year of operation:

(Projected expenses minus consulting income)   _____

State how you plan to cover the shortfall in income for the first year:

_____

_____

_____

NOTE: This is only one part of the financial picture. You have two more tasks to undertake before getting the full picture of what it takes to become a full-time, financially successful consultant. The first is to determine your first year operating costs and put together a list of fixed assets you will need sooner or later to build a consulting business. The second is to determine what your billing rate should be.

Part Two: Expenditure estimates for the initial year of full-time consulting

Part One provided the expenditures you would normally incur based on your current year's expenses. While it is a good start toward putting together a projected operating budget, you also will need to calculate your costs of starting up and running your own business. The next two worksheets will help you think through your first year's expenses *beyond the budget you have just completed.* The first is a proposed operating budget and the second a fixed asset budget. The latter is intended to cover equipment and other items you might want to amortize over a longer period of time. If so, you will need to determine the amortization schedule and break these costs down into yearly estimates.

Part Two: A: Operating Expenses

The following worksheet provides a column for estimates of only your first year's expenditures on a yearly basis. It will be helpful to break down these annual estimates into monthly estimates.

- Office rental   _____
- Non-reimbursable transportation   _____
- Utilities (i.e., electric)   _____
- Telephone/Internet   _____
- Legal fees, licenses   _____

- Clerical support _____
- Copying and printing _____
- Advertising and marketing _____
- Resource books, software _____
- Insurance _____
- Meals, entertainment _____
- Interest on loans, if necessary _____
- Postage _____
- Office supplies _____
- Business related taxes _____
- Repairs and maintenance _____
- Professional development _____
- _____ _____
- _____ _____

Total _____

Part Two: B: Fixed assets

The following is a list of some of the furniture and equipment you may need in order to operate effectively. While many consultants begin their career by working from their home or some other cost-cutting arrangement, it is nevertheless useful to think about what kind of office, furnishings, and equipment you will need and how you will factor these costs into your fees and contracts. While you may want to amortize these cost over several years, or defer as many as you can until later, it is important to consider the financial consequences of these expenditures as you plan for your decision to become a full-time consultant.

Basic equipment and furniture needs: The following is a list of some basic furniture and equipment you might find in a start-up consulting office. Check those you think you will need immediately and those you can delay purchasing until a later time. Also add any items that may be missing.

Equipment:	Buy now:	Buy later:	Estimated costs:
Notebook computer:	____	____	_____
Desktop computer:	____	____	_____
Telephone:	____	____	_____
Fax:	____	____	_____
Internet access:	____	____	_____
Printer:	____	____	_____
Copier:	____	____	_____
Easel (flipchart stand):	____	____	_____
_____	____	____	_____
_____	____	____	_____
Furniture:			
Desk:	____	____	_____
Chair:	____	____	_____
Worktables:	____	____	_____
File cabinets:	____	____	_____
Book shelves:	____	____	_____
_____	____	____	_____
_____	____	____	_____
Total:	____	____	_____

Decide the timeframe over which you plan to make these purchases and determine how you plan to recoup these costs in your consulting fees. Enter the details of your plans below.

_____

_____

_____

_____

Other less obvious but important costs: Many other costs involved in becoming self-employed aren't so obvious to those who are securely employed. For example, you will need to incorporate into your daily fee or contracts those non-monetary benefits you may have been receiving from your current employer: paid vacation, downtime due to illness (sick leave), holidays, and professional development opportunities such as attending conferences or workshops. For budgeting purposes, it helps to put a monetary amount on each of these benefits. Insert them below as part of your financial record.

These worksheets should provide a realistic look at the cost of doing business as a consultant. Not all of the costs may be applicable immediately; or, you may feel that some of them won't apply to your situation. Nevertheless, they provide valuable insights into the financial consequences of becoming a full-time consultant.

The Revenue Realities of Full-Time Consulting

Before completing the revenue side of the ledger, it is useful to look at some of the financial realities of full-time consulting.

The strategic, long-term view: A very few consultants get rich, many make a good living, others say it's the lifestyle choice that consulting offers and not the money that appeals to them, and some fail. Those who get rich, more often than not, write books and engage in media appearances to promote their theories and exploits. Those who make a good living from their consulting work have become specialists in the type of consulting services they offer. This specialization could be in one of the technical fields, like financial, engineering or marketing; or, it might be an example of process consulting, where their interpersonal, group, and organization knowledge and skills are directed to help others become better decision makers and problem solvers. For some, the life style is more important than making money. They like being "their own boss" and not having to punch a time clock.

Tactical, short-term realities

If you have been working for an established organization, don't automatically expect that your new clients will be interested in, or able to pay, consulting rates equivalent to what you were making with your current employer.

- You will need to make allowances for inevitable delays in payments and, on occasion, non-payment for services rendered.

- In spite of what you decide your daily rate should be, prepare to be flexible.

- If you don't have an overhead rate you can charge the client or the client doesn't accept paying overhead, have an agreement that covers expenses in addition to your daily rate.

- Some clients assume that all individual consultants are part-time consultants who have other full-time jobs. As a result the fees they set for consultants do not reflect such realities as vacations, medical down-time, holidays, and other costs that have to be borne by full-time consultants. Government agencies are notorious for this practice. While you may not be able to do anything about this institutional discrimination against full-time consultants, be aware that it exists.

- Your fees will be determined, in large measure, by the market place and your competitors. Before you commit to a career as a full-time consultant, check out the market place and your competition. What you think you are worth and what your prospective clients are willing to pay for your services may be vastly different.

- You may be confronted with the reality of choosing between never compromising on the daily rate you should be paid based on your billing rate calculations and keeping busy at a lower rate. Some consultants prefer to work fewer days at a higher rate while others opt for working many more days at a lower rate. Higher rates normally require more marketing time unless you are well-known and in demand. Lower rates expand the size of your market and usually require less marketing. It depends on how you like to spend your time. We personally have preferred to keep busy working at a lower rate than many we consider to be our professional equals in the business. As a result, we rarely have needed to spend time marketing our services.

- Talk to a few consultants who work in the same or similar areas of consulting on which you plan to concentrate. Add their thoughts to these reality checks before you make the final decision.

Options for billing clients

As a full-time consultant you will need to bill clients for your time and services. There are several options:

- *Fixed price contract*: you agree to perform certain mutually defined services or products for a fixed amount of money. This option usually means more risk for the consultant than the client. Delays, interruptions, unforeseen barriers: all can consume valuable time that was not budgeted. On the other hand, there is the opportunity to make a "profit" if you are able to finish the work in fewer days than either you or the client thought it would take when you agreed on the contract.

- *Fixed price plus expenses*: important when you don't know what expenses you might incur.

- *Daily rate plus expenses*: this is the most common billing option for individual consultants. As mentioned earlier, the decision about what your daily rate will be is not totally within your control. More about this later.

- *Retentions*: the client wants to have your services "on-call." In other words, the client is willing to pay a monthly or yearly fee to assure that your services can be tapped at any time. This arrangement is rarely used with individual consultants unless they are highly regarded by their clients and in high demand. There are risks for the consultant who overestimates the demand for his or her services.

- Other billing options exist, such as cost plus incentive fees, performance contracts, and costs plus a fixed fee, but it is rare for new consultants to encounter the need to go beyond those outlined above.

In spite of the variety of possibilities consultants have for billing their clients, most base their income and billings on a daily fee. This daily fee is based on the number of billable days they determine they have to work for clients, after calculating all the time they need for marketing, vacations, downtime, etc.

You were encouraged earlier to conduct a financial reality check to determine the amount of money you will need to make as a full-time consultant and to cover the operating and capital costs of starting and conducting a new business. These calculations represent the expenditure side of your budget. If you didn't perform these tasks and you are serious about becoming a full-time consultant, return to them immediately. Exceptions to this task include the independently wealthy and the brain dead.

Completing the revenue side of your budget

In order to balance the proposed expenditure side of the budget for the first twelve months of your new business and career, you need to deal with two important revenue variables.

The first is the number of days in the year that realistically are available for consulting. This is known in the trade as *billable days*.

The second variable is how much you will need to charge for your services on a daily basis to cover your personal and business costs for the year. Also include in the daily fee whatever profit you believe is important to maintaining your lifestyle or essential for building a business. This is known as your *billing rate*.

If you have been fully employed by someone else on a salary basis, you may be tempted to divide the total of your current or most recent salary into 260 days, or 52 weeks x five days per week. Don't! You now have to think in terms of *billable days.*

How to calculate billable days: *Warning!* This task may be depressing. Nevertheless, here is a suggested formula to use in determining the number of billable days in a year. Certain assumptions have been made that may not be the norm you plan to follow, such as allowing for vacation. In addition, you might want to vary the days allotted to other functions. Recalculate them to best reflect your situation and anticipated needs.

1. Number of days in the year	365
2. Subtract weekends (2x52): unless you plan to work weekends	-104
Sub-total	**261**
3. Subtract vacation and holidays: 20 vacation days + 10 holidays	-30
4. Subtract time for medical and emergency reasons: 10 days	-10
Sub-total	**221**
5. Subtract time needed for administrative work: average of 2 days/month	-24
6. And marketing: average of 3 days per month	-36
7. Downtime: for travel, running errands, cancelled or rescheduled assignments	-20
Total billable days:	**141**

Calculate your daily fee: Take the amount of money you think you will need for the first year of operation and divide it by the number of billable days you have calculated. This is the billing rate per day you will need to charge to balance your budget.

Note!: Be sure that you have included in your expenditure side of the budget all those costs associated with being self-employed. For example, did you include office rent, if applicable; utilities; telephone and internet charges; insurance; business promotion; photocopying and other office costs; non-reimbursable travel; etc.? These overhead costs must be built into your billable rate. Otherwise, you quickly will be sinking into debt.

How will you cope with *billable day* depression?

Many consultants get very depressed when they calculate how many billable days they have and realize how much they must charge per day to meet their budget. The reality is that most non-consultants do not appreciate how difficult it is to make a respectable living as a consultant. They rarely think about the monetary value of all the fringe benefits that come with working for an established employer.

However, there is good news. It is possible to be financially success-ful as a full-time consultant. Many consultants are, but first they must come to terms with the billable day syndrome. Here are some clues on how to do this.

- Realize what your billable rate should be but don't be chained to it. While you are marketing your services to get your calcu-lated daily rate, you could be working for less. In other words, you probably will not have to spend as much time marketing your body if you charge a lower daily rate. It depends on how you want to spend the time available.

- Go for longer consulting assignments, even if the rate is lower than you believe you should be paid. Sometimes, the client will allow you to bill on a six-day-a-week basis on longer contracts. This is often true for overseas assignments where there is a per diem living cost added to the contract.

- Take care of administrative chores, like paying bills and billing clients, in the evening or on weekends so they don't take time from consulting days.

- Market smart. It is very easy to waste time on reluctant and dubious clients.

- Concentrate on consulting assignments where your daily rate is less of a problem for the client. For example, conduct a training session and break the costs down into the cost per participant.

- Teach an evening course at the local university. It may not pay much, but consider it as additional income. The potential value-added dimensions include the possibility of meeting new future clients and adding to your own professional development.

- Cut your costs wherever you can. Money saved can be equiva-lent to money earned when you are in business for yourself.

- Develop materials you can sell to your clients.

- Plan to take your vacation when business is usually slow. Or, plan to take unscheduled, short vacations as obvious or not-so-obvious downtimes occur in your schedule.

- Link up with a larger consulting firm that may be able to use you on short notice for short assignments.

- Put a value on the non-monetary benefits of being an independent consultant. Money isn't everything. Many consultants are willing to risk making less money than they would on a regular job because they like the lifestyle and freedom.

- Exchange your services for services or goods you need. For example, conduct a management audit for a local automobile dealer in exchange for a discount on a new vehicle.

- Team up with other independent consultants to bid on assignments you can't handle alone.

- Establish long-term relationships with a few valued clients and be prepared to cut your fees when necessary to assure future contracts.

- Help clients be more successful as a result of your relationship with them. Most consultants look to their clients for references to new clients. Consultants can also refer their clients to others to help them grow their businesses.

- Establish a network of contacts that can help you build your business while you help them in return. Networks work best when there are opportunities for reciprocal benefits to all concerned.

- Write proposals during your downtime, but only write proposals that have a good chance of being funded. This option will be described later.

- Take time to reflect on all the non-monetary rewards that come with being a free-lance consultant.

Getting Specialized Help, Staying Legal, and Keeping Current.

Establishing and sustaining a consulting business often requires help from other professionals. Since most of these requirements will have an impact on your financial resources, this is the time to factor them into your plans.

Getting specialized help might be important in the following areas:

- Legal: On such things as writing contracts; knowing what laws you need to adhere to in your new business; and getting an overdue account paid from a reluctant client.

- Financial: To help you set up a simple double book-keeping system or to assist in determining what your overhead should be, based on accepted norms in your area and type of consulting business. Your fees might vary substantially, depending on your client. An accounting firm with a wide range of clients might be able to provide some valuable insights into this conundrum.

- Marketing and advertising: While most of your marketing and advertising will probably be conducted personally, there may be times when it helps to work with a professional in these fields.

- Depending on how your consulting business develops, you may require other kinds of specialized assistance.

Staying legal might require you to:

- register your new business;

- adhere to zoning requirements when establishing your business location;

- purchase various permits, depending on local laws and traditions;

- get a business identification number;

- obtain a business license;

- respect trademarks, copyrights, and patents;

- take out various kinds of insurance, particularly if you hire others;

- and pay various kinds of taxes.

- _____ (any others you can think of)

The legal requirements for establishing and operating a new business like consulting vary from location to location. The examples are designed to raise your awareness about possible legal implications of starting a new business. They are not intended as a definitive list.

While your lawyer or accountant can often provide this essential information, you also can learn about these requirements from well-established consultants and from the agencies requiring the licenses and permits. You will need to weigh the cost of getting professional help from an accountant or lawyer versus the cost of your time in tracking down the information on your own.

Keeping professionally current in your chosen field of consultancy will be important to the long-term sustainability and competitiveness of your business. There are lots of ways to keep your competitive edge as a professional consultant. To approach this task systematically, put together a professional development plan. Start with the Consulting Aptitude Inventory provided earlier and determine what areas of development might be useful to prepare you for the rigors of the consulting profession. Also think about:

- holding discussions with professional and personal friends who are willing to provide insights on what areas of personal and professional development they believe you should focus;

- joining a professional organization for enlightenment and contacts;

- subscribing to professional journals in your specific field;

- writing articles for a professional journal or other publications;

- attending conferences and workshops—to get the most leverage, attend as a presenter or workshop conductor;

- surfing the internet for ideas and tools by simply typing into a search engine the name of the topic in which you are interested;

- talking to those who are successful in consulting, and a few who haven't been;

- teaming up with a specialist who has different skills, knowledge, and experience;

- reading as much as you can about your particular specialty;

- taking on assignments that force you to grow in order to be successful in carrying them out; and

- adding to your formal education by attending academic courses and pursuing an additional academic degree.

- _____ (add your favorite way of learning)

Professional development can be expensive, especially if you rely on traditional approaches. Many consultants keep current and develop new professional skills and knowledge through on-the-job experiences and by developing a working library. Be creative in finding your professional development opportunities. Make your professional growth, and the development of those you might employ, an essential part of your consulting business.

Moving Right Along

After all these rigorous financial planning tasks, it is time to think about how you will market your services. Since developing a business plan for your new consulting business may be both an important tool for obtaining front-end funding for certain fixed and operating costs and an integral part of your marketing plan, we will look at this task first under the *Marketing* challenge.

Marketing takes a day to learn...
and a life time to master.

Philip Kotler

III. The *Marketing and Business Development* Challenge

What you can expect to find in this chapter:

- How to prepare a business plan
- What to include in your business plan
- Demand and supply perspectives on your marketing potential
- Direct and indirect marketing tactics
- The relationship factors in developing a successful marketing plan

---

As just noted we will start out looking at the business plan as one of the key marketing and business development documents, recognizing that writing the plan may be your best marketing strategy. It will help you to understand quickly who you are as a consultant and how you either operate now or plan to operate in the future. Beyond this, there is a look at how to determine market potential from supply and demand driven perspectives; direct and indirect marketing tactics; the importance of building and sustaining relationships as an integral part of your marketing strategy; needs assessment strategies; the role of proposal writing and marketing; and the dubious art of chasing client-driven requests for proposals (RFPs).

Preparing a Business Plan

It can be argued that many initial consulting efforts don't need a formal business plan. Many consultants operate successfully without one. Nevertheless, you will need one if you pursue competitive bid contracts, seek longer term client relationships, or need to borrow money to start your consulting practice. Business plans are also good marketing tools. Finally, preparing a business plan brings an added assurance that you have answered in a more formal way all the questions raised earlier about starting a consulting business.

Most publications on starting a consulting business include something on how to prepare a business plan. While many of these "how-to" books or manuals are similar in format, there are differences. The following is a synthesis of some of the more useful ideas gleaned from a variety of these publications. Take the ideas that best fit your emerging business situation and the context within which you plan to operate. Toss the others in the waste basket. While some of the points are obvious, like a cover page, we've included them so you get the whole picture.

Most business plans include the following:

- **Cover page**: self-evident but remember to include name of your new consulting business; a logo if you have one; contact person, address, telephone and fax numbers; and e-mail and web site addresses, if applicable. Some authors also advise to add a date. Your cover page is the first impression your client will have of the business plan that follows, so it is important.

- **Table of contents**.

- **Executive summary** or introductory statement.

- **A mission statement** for your new enterprise. The mission statement should say in a few short sentences what your business does—your purpose as a new enterprise. It could be as simple as: Our mission is to provide quality consulting services to small businesses and non-governmental organizations, at competitive prices, in the areas of management and organization development.

- Also, consider including a **vision statement.** This is a statement of what you hope to achieve over a longer period of time by carrying out your mission. For example, what levels of success do you see your new enterprise achieving in three to five years? Future success can be described in many ways, e.g., increased revenue, size of your professional staff, depth and breadth of clients—in other words, by those criteria that are important to you and your organization.

- **Short term and longer range goals and objectives**. These might include financial goals for the first year and a five year projection; growth in the size and impact of your new consultation business by, for example, adding two full-time consultants within three years; linking with a large on-going project to provide capacity building services to specific clientele. Goals and objectives are your roadmap into the future.

- **Organization template and operational plan**. This might include any alliances you already have or consortiums of consultants you can team with to provide services in the future. Often individual consultants establish networks of individuals who can offer a variety of services so collectively they can be more competitive in pursuing contracts. If you plan to grow substantially and anticipate adding new staff, then this should be reflected in this statement.

- Your **credentials and a description of the services** you are offering now and plan to offer in the future. Be as specific as possible so those reading your plan will understand the scope of services you offer, or will offer. These might include technical consulting services on helping organizations establish new budgeting systems; workshops on communications; assistance in planning and managing conferences; in-house staff development programs; etc.

- **Market analysis and market focus**. Include information like the types of clients you currently serve, or plan to serve; the size and demographics of these markets; their potential and willingness to purchase consulting assistance; the status of your competition and how your new organization will work within that competitive field to gain a planned market share.

- **Your marketing strategy**: How do you define your market? What geographic areas and types of organizations do you plan to target in your marketing initiatives? What marketing strategies, including advertising and promotions, do you plan to use in building your business? Do you plan to use professional marketing services to increase your exposure? Your strategy might involve indirect marketing strategies, such as active involvement in professional associations or service organizations.

- **The risks** you might be confronted with in conducting your business over a sustained period. This is the type of information that funding agencies and clients might find useful, particularly clients who want to establish a long term relationship. If, for example, you are heavily dependent on business from an organization you recently worked for, what are your plans to minimize the risks of being dependent on that organization over time?

- Closely aligned to marketing are **your pricing strategies.** How do you plan to charge for your services, and how did you arrive at these decisions? This section might also include information on overhead rates, a breakdown of your daily fees, and any other assumptions about how you plan to operate financially that will be helpful to prospective clients or funding organizations.

- **Your management plan**. If you are a lone entrepreneur, this might include such information as how you plan to manage all the administrative and financial aspects of your new business; what experience you have in managing a small business; what professional help you will use, such as legal, accounting and more specialized needs; and the status of your banking services. This could be as simple as assuring clients that you can provide information for electronic transfers of funds.

- **Supporting documentation**, including resumes of key people, a detailed financial statement when necessary, letters of external support, and examples of key services.

From a review of the literature, it is obvious that there are no standard templates to compile a business plan. Given this, it might be helpful to talk to key individuals who potentially could be recipients of your business plan.

Writing a business plan may not be the most important thing to do in the start-up phase of your new business. On the other hand, putting together a plan, based on this outline, can be an important learning experience, unearthing many issues you may not think of otherwise. So do it.

Determining Market Potential from Two Perspectives: Demand and Supply

Building a successful consulting business depends on many things. Being able to tap the market potential is among the most important. Without a market for their services, consultants have little reason to exist. It is important to understand how to market your services, and how to exploit the market potentials that exist for your services, if you plan to be successful as a consultant.

The consulting market is both demand driven and supply driven. Clients have a demand for your services and seek you out. Or, you, as a consultant, help the client understand why he needs your services. To be successful you will need to work both sides of the supply and demand market potential. You also need to know the differences between direct and in-direct marketing tactics and strategies and how to exploit both.

Client needs and desires: the demand side of market potential

Most consultants start with what they can do and try to find clients who might need their services. This is supply driven marketing. There is nothing wrong with this approach and it will be addressed shortly. But first, it is important to look at why clients need and want consultant services. For example, the client:

- is experiencing staff shortages, i.e., short term, seasonal, or even long term, and needs a consultant to fill the gap;

- needs an objective, outside assessment of some aspect of the organization and its operation and calls in a consultant to undertake the assessment;

- has just learned there are new government regulations her organization will be responsible for implementing and calls a consultant to conduct a workshop on how to comply to the new regulations;

- is experiencing a budget crisis and needs to explore ways to minimize the consequences to the organization and citizens;

- needs a second opinion on a new operating software before adopting it;

- is eligible for grants that are available through an international foundation and needs help in putting together the grant proposal;

- wants to provide communication training for the service staff who interact with the public; or,

- needs help in understanding and appreciating how their organization can use the services of consultants more effectively in implementing their mission.

Since consulting businesses are built on the needs of clients for their services, it is important to understand why they might need your services. What drives clients to spend scarce resources on consultants? Client-driven demands will, in large measure, define your success as a consultant.

How you tap into that demand is your next challenge in determining the market for your services. You need to determine the niche within the wide spectrum of client-driven demands for consulting services that match your capacity to deliver. This is where the business plan you have put together will be invaluable. Who do you want to be as a consultant? And, how does this fit with what you know about the needs of your potential clients for this kind of consulting services? *The market potential for your services depends largely on matching who you are, or who you want to be as a successful consultant, with the right niche in the client-driven market for your services.*

More client-driven factors to consider

While determining your niche within the client-driven demands for consulting services will be central to your success as a consultant, there are other demand-driven factors to consider. For example, if you decide your client focus will be developing financial management systems for small businesses and non-governmental organizations (NGOs), you also will need answers to the following questions.

- Will they have money to spend on this type of consulting service if there is no external support funding available?

- Even if they have the funds, will they be willing to spend it on my services?

- How many small businesses and NGOs would be able, and willing, to buy my services in developing financial management systems?

- Are they geographically situated so I can serve them easily?

- How much competition will there be from other consultants who can provide similar services?

- How much credibility will I have with these potential clients and their decision-makers?

- How easy will it be for me to communicate with those who will be making the decision to use my services?

- _____(add your own client-driven questions to these when putting together your marketing plan)

Consulting capacity: the supply side of marketing potential

Probably as many businesses are built on supply side marketing as client-driven needs. The following factors will be important in working from the supply side to build your consulting business.

- Narrow your client focus and define your niche within that client focus.

- Know your clients and their needs, constraints, values, and aspirations.

- Anticipate what their future needs might be for your services. Sometimes this is as simple as knowing what new demands, such as changes in government regulations that might require your help in interpreting and implementing.

- Know what you can deliver with a high level of personal and organizational confidence. Overselling who you are and what you can do usually happens only once per client. Underselling who you are and what you can do rarely results in a contract for your services.

- Be motivated. Convey to your clients, in whatever way is appropriate, that you want their business.

- Learn how to work effectively within the culture of the client systems you are pursuing.

- Be realistic in your pricing policies.

- Be able to explain what you can do for your client in a one page letter or a five minute phone call.

- _____(add your own ideas about supply-side marketing)

Direct and Indirect Marketing Tactics

Think of the ideas and insights just discussed as marketing strategies. Within these are a wide range of marketing tactics you can use to increase the visibility of your new business. They fall roughly into two categories: direct marketing tactics and those that are indirect. **Direct marketing tactics include such activities as**:

- Making direct contact with potential clients and following up on these contacts.

- Asking for references from current clients and others and pursuing them with phone calls or letters.

- Sending out letters and brochures about your services and following up on the mailings with personal contacts.

- Keeping in touch with prospective clients through e-mail exchanges.

- Advertising through various media.

- Hosting an open house event for prospective clients to introduce your business and contacting again those who attend.

- Focusing advertising efforts on a specific management consulting service with a broad market appeal, such as strategic planning or team building.

- Setting up a web-site and following up on leads.

- Preparing a marketing kit with descriptions of your services, contacts, and other useful information and distributing them in high traffic locations.

- Setting up a booth at national and regional meetings and conferences where prospective clients might attend and contacting soon after those prospective clients who show interest in your services.

- Working through an advertising firm—but only if you get desperate.

- Preparing personal and business resumes that describe who you are, what you have done, and what you can do. These resumes should reflect local customs in their preparation. If all fails, buy a book on writing effective resumes.

- Using attractive stationary, business cards, and other printed materials that convey professionalism.

- Developing a newsletter to send to key clients and prospective clients. Ask for feedback to incorporate into the next issue of the newsletter. Follow up with those who respond. They could be future clients.

- Registering with governments, aid agencies, and other organizations that issue written requests for proposals for the types of services you are offering.

- Scanning the major newspapers for legal announcements on services to be purchased through some type of formal bidding process.

- _____(add to this list those direct approaches to marketing that you believe might be effective in your circumstances)

Each of these suggested direct approaches to marketing must be considered from several perspectives.

1. Are they appropriate within the context of your anticipated market area?

2. How effective will they be in relation to other approaches?

3. What will the costs be in relation to potential business?

Some Final Thoughts about Direct Marketing Tactics

- Direct advertising is, generally, the least effective and most expensive marketing tactic for small start-up professional businesses like consulting. Consider it a tactic of last resort.

- Direct referrals from satisfied and respected clients can be among the most productive direct marketing tactics. They rarely happen without effort on your part. Ask your valued clients for their advice, ideas, and contacts. Thank them sincerely for their references and follow up immediately on their efforts to be helpful.

- Responding to formal requests for proposals (RFPs) can also be effective if you are established and can afford the time and costs associated with formal bidding processes. Since there is usually a lot of competition for competitively bid contracts, this may have to wait until your business is firmly established and you can risk the time and resources necessary to prepare all the bid documents. An alternative is to become either a sub-contractor in another proposal or an expert who can be called upon to provide services as part of the winner's team. While many firms want an exclusive from individual experts/consultants, many are willing to waive this requirement if you are highly valued by many.

- Have a marketing kit available with resumes, business cards, service descriptions, and other pertinent materials that you can give potential clients at professional meetings and other contact situations.

- Follow-up, follow-up, follow-up. While this marketing strategy has been emphasized repeatedly, it is at the core of every consultant's success.

Indirect marketing tactics include a vast array of activities and initiatives. Among the most common are:

- Attending professional meetings and conferences to meet prospective clients.

- Joining local civic and service organizations.

- Making presentations at professional association conferences and civic events.

- Writing a column for your local newspaper.

- Meeting with other consultants to exchange ideas and contacts. They may be working with different client groups and providing different services than you do, so there would be little if any competition involved.

- Writing articles for professional journals, newspapers, and publications.

- Offering to conduct short (1-4) hour workshops for employees of prospective clients.

- Sponsoring a community event, such as a charity marathon run.

- Sharing your expertise freely with others, including other consultants.

- Teaching a continuing education course at a local college or university.

- Creating an advisory group of client representatives to provide feedback on current services and new consulting opportunities.

- _____ (include one or more of the most interesting and in-direct marketing tactics you have heard of recently)

Most consultants use a variety of indirect marketing techniques to keep their name in front of prospective clients. Many resemble something called "networking." Networking involves keeping in regular contact with an ever-widening circle of friends and business acquaintances who can provide information and insights that could result in new business. Networking, as a business development resource, has gotten easier with the advent of e-mail, cell phones, and web-sites.

Marketing Is About Relationships

Anthony Putman, in his book *Marketing Your Services*, offers some sage advice on marketing. He says marketing is not advertising, nor promotion, nor sales. *Marketing is a set of lenses you use to look at your business— your entire business.* Putman goes on to say that effective *marketing concentrates on one thing only: the relationship between your business and its market.* (1990, p.5)

Creating and maintaining **the client-consultant relationship**, according to Putman, is an intentional process of being able to say what you can do and doing it. It involves:

- Making a commitment to be in business in contrast to doing whatever happens to come along that looks interesting.

- Defining your business mission so that everyone, including you, knows exactly what you do. (Once again, the relevance and importance of developing a business plan is stressed, even if no one else sees it but you.)

- Identifying what is the best target market for your services. While "best" is always subjective, it is important to define this from your unique perspective, interests, and motivations.

- Causing your consulting business and its services to stand out from the crowd. This means, among other things, creating in the minds of your clients the perception that both you and the services you provide are distinctive and valuable.

- Creating a laser-like alignment between you and your target clientele. Alignment comes from getting all your energy focused in one direction—in making sure that everything you say and do is congruent and seen that way by your clients. (1990, p.10)

While all these actions about which Putman talks are integral to marketing, they also are important in building and sustaining consultant-client relationships generally. Putman just puts a marketing spin on them since that is his field of expertise.

Never express yourself more clearly
than you are able to think.

Niels Bohr

IV. The *Communicating* Challenge

What you can expect to find in this chapter:

- The importance and complexity of effective communication
- Effective listening strategies
- Asking the right kinds of questions
- Giving and receiving feedback
- Holding skillful discussions
- Making effective presentations
- The art of writing convincing reports
- Documentation

The Interpersonal Dimension of Successful Consulting

Communicating well and making sense of the verbal and non-verbal human interactions of others are essential consultant skills. While communicating is often described as the simple transfer of information from one person to another, it is not always that simple. Communicating is a mix of complex interactions involving facts, feelings, perceptions, innuendos, and many other things. It involves not only spoken or written messages but also gestures, physical posture, tone of voice, timing, and other non-verbal statements that can be very persuasive—or distractive.

In reality, much of what happens when people communicate takes place below the surface, where what is said is not necessarily what is meant. All too often the process is laden with a weird mix of ethnic, racial, religious, political, and gender nuances that haunt our ability to really understand what is being said. These filters make it difficult to easily access and process messages and information from each other.

When fuzzy communication takes place between you, as the consultant, and your client, be prepared to assume at least 50% of the blame.

Fortunately, there are many communication tools that consultants and clients can use to better understand and appreciate each other. These tools include active listening, perhaps our most important communication skill; asking questions that avoid dead-end discussions; giving and receiving feedback; and holding skillful dialogues. Before delving into these specific skills and tools, there is another perspective about the communication process that is important to consider.

The Johari Window of Missed Communicating Opportunities

More than four decades ago, two consultants discovered there was something missing in their communication with clients and others. As a result, Joseph Luft and Harry Ingham devised something they called the "Johari Window," a label that incorporated their first names. Their communication window has four panes in it, just like many common kitchen windows. And these panes represent some of the most important lessons to be learned about how we communicate, or don't. Here is a brief look through these four panes and what they mean in terms of the consultant-client relationship.

1. The *Open* pane: In the communication process, this is what is known to both the consultant and the client. It represents mutual understanding and shared information.

2. The *Blindspot* pane: This is what the client knows but isn't sharing with the consultant. What isn't being communicated could be important information in terms of their working relationship and efforts to engage in productive decision making and problem solving. For the consultant, this represents a blind-spot in the communication process.

3. The *Facade* pane: This is information and ideas the consultant has that could be useful to the goals of the consultancy but hasn't shared with the client for whatever reason. For example, some consultants hold back information to keep the client dependent on his or her continuing contributions. Or, the consultant may simply not be aware that he or she is not being open in communicating with the client.

4. The *Unknown* pane: This is the area of greatest potential—where latent creativity is quietly waiting to happen. More often than not, it's this unknown pane, or pain, that brings consultants and clients together. If you are an *expert* consultant, you are expected to know the answer to the client's problems. Unfortunately, it may not be self-evident without some enlightening communications between the two parties. For the *process* consultant, the challenge is to shrink the *blind-spot* and *facade* panes so the *open* pane can expand. When this happens, the unknown pane will diminish and on occasion disappear.

Working With the Johari Window As a Consultant

Expanding the open pane requires a number of communication skills. If the communication problems you and your client are experiencing are in the *Blindspot* or *Facade* panes, you have several options. You can elect to use *receptive* communicating skills to gather more information and to increase mutual understanding; or, you may choose to use *expressive* skills by sharing information in a direct and constructive manner.

McLagan and Krembs, two able consultants who manage to bounce between North America and South Africa with confidence, provide definitions for these communication tools.

Receptive communicating skills are comprised of:

- **Observing:** to notice more acutely what is going on.

- **Listening:** to actively attend to what is being said and to paraphrase what is being heard.

- **Empathizing:** to understand and validate the other person's experiences.

Expressive communicating skills include:

- **Questioning:** asking for information and insights in ways that get relevant and appropriate responses without putting the responder is a defensive mode.

- **Describing:** providing concrete and objective examples of what you see and how it affects the quality of the conversation.

- **Concluding:** bringing closure to discussions and making decisions to move on. (1995, pp. 52-60)

With this conceptual framework about the communication process and its importance to the success of consultant-client relationships and productivity firmly in mind, it's time to explore some of the communication skills and tools in more depth. Of all the communicating tools and skills required to be an effective consultant, active listening is undoubtedly the most important.

The Art of Active Listening

The mark of an effective client-consultant relationship is how well they listen to one another. It is by listening that a consultant gets a true picture of a client's interests, wants, and concerns. Many of the problems that arise later in a consulting relationship are caused by information gaps resulting from listener inattention, distraction, or preoccupation during early conversations.

When a listener is giving her full attention to the dynamics of a conversation, she is engaged in "active" listening. Listening actively is more than just paying close attention to what is being said. If that was the only skill being used, a transcript of the conversation would do as well. By watching closely for cues, like the speaker's tone of voice and body language, the active listener can pick up far more insight from a conversation than a passive listener can.

Here are a few examples of *active listening* skills in action:

- You can express interest in what the client is saying by simply responding, "*I see!*"

- To encourage the client to expand on his thinking, you might say, "*Yes, tell me more.*"

- To help the client clarify a problem, you might say, "*Then, the problem as you see it is…*"

- To get the client to clarify what she has said, you might say, "*If I understand you correctly, you are saying we should…*" In the communication business, this is known as paraphrasing.

- To pull the key ideas out of a long statement or discussion, you might engage in some descriptive expressions like, "*Your main point is…*" or "*You feel we should…*"

- To respond to a client's feelings more than to the words spoken, you might say, *"You feel strongly about that..."*

- To summarize some of the key points in reaching an agreement with your client, you might say, *"We seem to be agreed on the following points..."* or *"It seems we need further clarification on the last two..."*

Key Components of Successful Listening

Since listening is the consultant's most important communication ally, here are a few additional insights on this common consulting tool. Successful listening is the product of four key skills: hearing the message; interpreting the message; evaluating the message; and responding to the message.

1. **Hearing the message** is hampered by the following barriers. Take a moment and check off the barriers you are most guilty of using when listening to your clients.

   - Thinking about other things.   _____

   - Letting emotions get in my way.   _____

   - Disagreeing with my client.   _____

   - Listening for flaws in my client's logic.   _____

   - Thinking about how I will respond.   _____

   - Wanting to express my own ideas.   _____

   - Feeling some kind of prejudice.   _____

   - Interpreting what the client is saying.   _____

   - Letting outside distractions interfere.   _____

   Since listening effectively to your clients is so important, spend a few moments thinking about those barriers you just checked. Jot down some ideas of what you can do to take down these barriers in your next client discussion.

_____

_____

_____

2. **Interpreting the message** is the skill of coming to a mutual understanding about what the client or consultant means by what is being said. Achieving this mutual understanding is not easy since we rarely perceive things in exactly the same way. Many of the statements presented above are designed to help in the interpretation stage of effective listening. It will be helpful to return to those statements and check those that are associated with *interpreting other people's messages.*

The interpreting stage of active listening includes such communicating skills as:

- paraphrasing what the client said;

- pulling key points from the client's discussion and reflecting them back for emphasis;

- encouraging the client to expand on his or her thinking;

- probing for more meaning on those ideas you don't quite understand;

- looking for non-verbal cues that might even tell you more than the spoken message; and

- asking for clarification. When in doubt, ask for more information.

3. **Evaluating the message** is the stage where the listener can get in trouble if this skill is used indiscriminately. The challenge is in knowing the difference between *evaluating* what the person is saying and making a value judgment. For example, *"Let me see if I understand what you just said..."* is preferable to *"That's a dumb idea. No wonder you need help!"*

4. **Responding to what your client has to say** is essential. This part of the active listening process is letting the other person know that the message was heard, understood, and evaluated. After all, you want to reach a mutual understanding and agreement so that you can move beyond this "contracting" stage of the consultation.

Asking Questions

Your task as a consultant is to solve problems for clients or help clients solve their own problems. To get the information needed to be helpful, a consultant must ask questions. That may seem obvious enough, but there is an art to asking questions. A well thought out and artfully stated question is a wonder to behold. For example, it can:

1. surface information you will need to help the client solve her problem;

2. help the client to see a problem from a different perspective;

3. test for misunderstandings that might otherwise derail the relationship; and

4. demonstrate understanding about the client's situation.

If you see some similarity between the active listening tools and these questioning tools, don't be dismayed. Effective conversations and dialogues are a rich mix of active listening and challenging questions. However, it is important to understand there is a big difference between challenging questions and confrontational questions. The following types of questions are those you will want to use in forging and maintaining positive and productive consultant-client relationships. They come in a variety of sizes, shapes, and purposes.

- **Essential Questions** are designed to provide an organizing focus for a conversation or inquiry. *What will it take to raise the literacy rate of our school children?*

- **Probing Questions** are designed to dig deeper into the subject of a conversation or inquiry. *Could you tell me more about that?*

- **Clarifying Questions** are designed to verify the accuracy of a statement that otherwise might be misinterpreted. *What exactly do you mean by "My boss is impossible"?*

- **Elaborating Questions** are designed to explore the possible implications of a statement. *What might happen if we continue in this direction?*

- **Sorting-out Questions** are designed to identify what is most relevant and useful from a large body of information. *What parts of the data we have collected are worth keeping?*

- **Planning Questions** are designed to identify the resources needed to achieve an intended purpose. *Who is best equipped to provide the needed leadership?*

- **Organizing Questions** are designed to structure information into categories from which we can determine patterns and relationships. *How much time should we allow for each task?*

- **Hypothetical Questions** are designed to stimulate thinking about possibilities or consequences. *What's the worst that could happen if we delay moving ahead?*

- **Provocative Questions** are designed to challenge conventional wisdom and give free rein to doubt, disbelief, and skepticism. *What could be the unintended consequences of this proposed action?*

Use of these nine questions can help move an inquiry about client problems and needs productively forward and upward. Other questions may have the opposite effect. **Closed-ended questions**, which produce "yes" or "no" answers, can stop a conversation dead in its tracks. **Leading questions** that begin with words like "Don't you think..." may come across as manipulative or self-serving, and **hostile** questions like "WHAT do you MEAN by THAT?!" may be interpreted by a client as a personal attack.

Asking appropriate questions, avoiding misunderstandings, and encouraging creative thinking are among the most valuable skills in the consultant's tool kit.

Giving and Receiving Feedback

Earlier in the discussion of the Johari Window, we pointed out that our ability to work together to solve problems or make decisions is dependent on our willingness to share openly what we know and feel. Feedback is a communication process designed to bring information about a situation from someone who has access to it to the attention of someone who does not.

Giving feedback. Giving feedback under the right circumstances can have many individual and group benefits. It can make someone aware of behaviors that support the group in carrying out its tasks. It can also reveal behaviors that are not supportive and should be modified in some way. Feedback given early enough might solve a problem before it becomes a crisis event. When used regularly, feedback can help to build healthy and trusting relationships among people as they become more aware of where they stand with each other.

Giving feedback under the wrong circumstances, like giving bad advice, can be destructive. A manipulative person, for example, might use information at his or her disposal to distort the thinking or actions of someone else. Equally bad is someone giving feedback to a person who has not asked for it, particularly when the feedback is not in that person's best interest.

Keeping the following considerations in mind can enhance a person's effectiveness in giving useful and accurate feedback:

- *Make it specific.* Being clear about the information to be conveyed makes it easier for the other person to understand it and act on it. Vague generalities are not helpful.

- *Be direct.* Deliver the feedback yourself. No one wants to get the news via a third party, particularly if it is personal and not favorable.

- *Be timely.* Get the feedback to someone while there is still time to do something about it.

- *Be descriptive, not evaluative.* Name the behavior and its consequences for the person and others without attacking or ridiculing the person receiving the feedback.

- *Check for a response.* Be sure the message has been received and is understood.

- *Don't overlook the need for positive feedback.* If you operate on the assumption that no news is good news, your silence may be conveying the message that "you don't care." Positive feedback is just as important as commenting on areas of needed improvement.

Receiving feedback. If you are on the other end of the feedback, the receiving end, there are some things for you to keep in mind:

- *Don't become defensive.* While it may be hard to avoid defensiveness, particularly when the message is unfavorable, don't be so busy putting up defenses—the "yes, but..." routine—that the value of the feedback gets lost.

- *Take it for what it's worth.* Not everyone who gives feedback is skilled at doing it. So use what is valid and relevant to you and discard what is not.

- *Question the feedback.* Don't hesitate to ask clarifying questions when receiving feedback. Likewise, give the recipient the same opportunity if you are the one giving feedback.

There's More to Communicating Than Doing Your Person-to-Person Charm Offensive

We have spent a lot of time on some basic interpersonal communication skills for good reason! They are central to a profession like consulting. If you don't have your person-to-person communication act together, you probably won't last long as a free-lance consultant. But the interpersonal up-front ability to communicate effectively is just half the challenge. You also will need to document what you are doing and what happens in interactions with your clients. And, you will need to make presentations and write reports. The following is just a glimpse of the more formal aspects of communicating to expect when you hang out your *Consultant for Hire* sign.

The Importance of Documentation

Written proposals are just a part of the documentation process you will want to incorporate into your consulting business practices. To better understand what is important to put in writing, it helps to look at the overall need and desire for documentation from the perspectives of the client and the consultant.

From the client's perspective. Clients often expect the following things in writing from the consultant:

A personal resume detailing education, professional experience, and references.

- If you operate as an organization, a statement of what your company does.

- Written examples of your work.

- Articles you have written that are appropriate.

- Proposals based on previous discussions.

- A final signed agreement on what is to be done, who will be responsible for what, and other details of the agreed upon working relationship.

- Terms of reference detailing what you might do in a short intervention. (It is not uncommon for consultants to assist in writing terms of reference for specific assignments. It often helps to clarify what both sides want from the client-consultant interaction.)

- Interim and final reports based on the progress and outcomes of the intervention.

These documents generally follow the sequence of events that are common to most consulting relationships.

From the consultant's perspective. As a consultant you have two different types of documentation needs: one from the client and one from your own initiatives.

Depending on the type of intervention, you might need from the client documents like:

- Annual reports and other public relations type materials to help you become more familiar with the client.

- Internal staff reports that focus on issues associated with the agreed upon intervention.

- Financial reports if the consultation involves the financial well-being of the organization.

- Minutes of meetings where the consultancy was discussed.

In each of these cases, you need to be aware of the sensitivity of both asking for and receiving documentation from the client. Nevertheless, it is important to be fully informed about the history of the need for intervention and the forces surrounding the intervention. Without being as fully informed as possible, your potential contribution can be limited. This is one of those aspects in any consulting relationship when mutual trust becomes the guiding factor.

As a consultant who is serious about being successful in this business, you also will benefit from making and keeping records of key events in your experiences with clients. Think about it as a dog marking his territory. Here are a few examples of the kinds of documents that come in handy as you build a successful consulting business:

- Minutes of planning and other types of meetings with your clients.

- Copies of marked up proposals that turned out to be interim proposals. These can help you begin to track the types of issues and concerns clients have had regarding your proposals. (We've found such documents to be invaluable in helping us remember how we arrived at our final agreement on what is to be done in a consultancy as well as in helping us appreciate the importance of collaborative planning and decision making as we often muddle forward to a working agreement.)

- All business-related financial transactions, even though they are not reimbursable from the client. (While this seems like a self-evident truism, many consultants are ineffective record keepers.)

- Workshop and work session materials of all kinds. These are the tools of your trade. Often they can be modified and reused with other clients.

- Evaluation reports.

- At the completion of each consulting assignment, it is helpful to jot down the lessons learned from the experience as well as things you would do differently if you could start the consultancy over again.

- _____
  _____(add your own ideas on documentation)

About Those Client Reports

Most clients expect both interim and final reports on any consulting investment they make. It's good business. So plan on spending part of your life writing reports and a lesser but equally important part of your life making sure you get paid for writing time. That's also a good business practice but one many of us overlook.

Regarding **progress reports** to the client, here are a few guidelines to keep in mind:

- Be brief and timely. Long reports rarely get read by the right people, particularly if they long, rambling dissertations that arrive the day before an important holiday.

- Progress reports are just that—a highlight of progress being made along with lessons learned and potential new developments uncovered.

- Be candid and open about any problems you might have uncovered. While most clients don't like to hear about problems, they like even less not to be informed about them as soon as possible.

- Progress reports also should revisit any timeline that was initially established for your work with the client, be clear about the current status, and redefine the future timeline, if necessary, in concrete future action steps.

- This may be the time to make recommendations if they will affect the need for intermediate actions on your part or the part of your client.

Interim progress reports not only keep your client informed about what is happening, they provide you with the raw material needed to write the final report on your work with the client.

The content and style of **your final report** will depend on why you were hired and what you accomplished. It is safe to assume that most clients will want, in writing, a summary of conclusions and recommendations resulting from your consultancy and whether your continued involvement will be beneficial. Don't be shy about recommending additional assignments for your services. On the other hand, remember that effective consultants, particularly of the process variety, are supposed to work themselves out of business.

Content. The following is an outline of the kinds of things that most final reports would include once you get past the cover page and table of contents:

- **Executive summary**: A one-pager, or maybe two or three, stating the major conclusions and recommendations. Keep this succinct, big-picture-ish, and punchy. It may be the only part of the report that many executives up the line will read.

- **The rationale for the assignment:** Or *perspective* on the consultation. Why were your services needed and how, if it seems useful, was the decision made.

- **An overview of what took place:** A brief summary of the course of events that unfolded during the consultancy is always helpful to put the next part of the report into perspective.

- **Conclusions and recommendations:** This is the guts of the report—an elaboration of the points highlighted in the executive summary. Make sure these two parts of your report are consistent with each other. Don't hesitate to enrich this part of the report with information and ideas that will help the client and staff implement the conclusions and recommendations.

- **Implementation strategies:** It is not unusual for many consultancies to include an action planning session at the completion of the consultancy. If such a session is held with key stakeholders, then a copy of the action plan should be included in your report. If such a session has not been held, then consider including a section that covers issues of *where the client needs to go from here* in taking full advantage of your good work.

- **Appreciation stuff:** It's always nice to thank those who helped you make the consultancy successful. While it's listed to be included at the end, don't hesitate to move it up front.

Style. The style and presentation of your report also are important. As authors Nelson and Economy remind us, consultants are judged as much on how their reports look as on what they say. Here's a summary of what they have to say about the presentation of consulting reports (1997, pp.169-70):

- **Drafting and layout**: In the drafting, use a simple, uncomplicated sentence structure; avoid unfamiliar words that might be misunderstood or culturally sensitive words and expressions. Use plenty of white space, indentations, margins, headings, bulleted lists, and other layout features to make your reports appear more inviting to the reader. Ask your clients for examples of reports they like or check the word processing software you use for standardized report templates.

- **Graphics**: Graphs, tables, charts, photographs, drawings, and other graphical features make your reports more attractive and professional in appearance. But don't go overboard. Too many graphics can be distracting.

- **Proofreading**: Check the report draft closely for grammatical and typographical errors. As mentioned above, this will avoid you the embarrassment of having your work judged by a poorly proofread report.

- **Composition and printing**: Use a full-service computer word processing program and print the report out on a good quality laser printer.

- **Paper stock and covers**: Use a top-quality, heavyweight paper for the text. Most report covers used by consultants consist of a transparent front cover that both protects and provides easy access to the cover page of the report as well as a heavy, color-coordinated back cover.

- **Binding**: Use whatever binding is common and acceptable in your region to insure that your report reflects the quality of your professional services.

Writing and producing accurate, convincing, thorough, and professionally attractive reports of what transpires between you and your client during the consultancy is a **must-do** responsibility. If you find writing difficult or you have doubts about the quality of your written products, hire someone to edit your reports before they are presented to your client. Most communities have an abundance of qualified individuals—high school teachers, local reporters, or stay-at-home mothers—who can provide this kind of assistance at reasonable rates and who may welcome the opportunity to work with you on this key consulting task.

The Ubiquitous Presentation Challenge

Making effective presentations is an important part of consulting. You no doubt will be required to make one or more presentations to get the assignment, particularly with new clients. You also will be called upon during the consultancy to explain what you are doing. Finally, you will be expected to explain what you did to justify your fee when it's over. As you become successful, there may be opportunities to share your expertise and experiences at conferences or other public events. Giving effective presentations can be a factor in attracting new business. Presentations will become an integral part of your consulting work-style, so be prepared to make the most of them.

Here are a few general tips on how to make these presentations. They are directed to two general types of presentations: those internal to the organization where you working as a consultant and non-client presentation opportunities, such as addressing professional conferences. In either case, you will need to adapt your presentation to fit the purpose, circumstances, and audience being addressed.

- **Purpose**: With client presentations you will, in most cases, be able to determine the purpose of your presentation, e.g., progress report, summary of findings, etc. If you are invited to make a presentation to a non-client specific group, be sure to find out exactly why you have been invited. Ask questions about the nature of the meeting and the meeting organizer's expectations for the meeting and from your presentation. Get details about the audience size and composition, the venue, how much time you are being given, and the issue of compensation. It is important to have these details in advance and preferably in writing to avoid potential misunderstanding.

- **Audience**: Regarding client presentations, the audience will be important. If it is an operations team, they probably will want more specifics. If it is a top management briefing, they may be more interested in the big picture. In any presentation, client centered or otherwise, you need to know the audience.

- **Preparation:** Based on the purpose and the audience, your presentation plan should include presentation objectives; a strong opening that highlights the importance of the subject and its relevance for the audience; subject-centered content that is organized around no more than three key points; and an ending that closes by repeating what was introduced in the opening.

- **The venue:** The arrangement of chairs, the sound system, the lighting, and the overall climate of the room can make a big difference in the way a presentation is received. If you have prior access to the room where your presentation will be made, get there as early as possible. This will give you time to get familiar with the room layout, table and chair arrangement, and equipment setup. If there are problems with these or other things, you have time to get them corrected before the audience arrives. In staff briefings, it is helpful to have available either white boards or an easel and flip chart paper so you can capture key points in any interactions that take place.

- **Visuals:** Visual aids (power point presentations, overhead projection, displays on the wall, any of these) can add an important dimension to many presentations. They help to focus audience attention on key points being made and to eliminate fatigue from otherwise overlong presentations. Visuals create interest, add variety, and make a presentation more interesting—even memorable. Use visuals frequently. But be careful that visuals don't supplant the central focus of the presentation.

- **Opening:** The opening should clarify the purpose of your presentation and capture the audience's attention. With client presentations, the subject matter will—or should be—of interest to them. With non-client presentations, you will want to relate what you plan to say so you attract their attention from the beginning. Sharing an experience of your own is one way to do that. Or start with an attention-getting statement such as, "Your job won't exist five years from now." Illustrate your points—how it is now, how it will or could be—with a story so vivid that the audience can "see" it. Asking questions is imperative to any client presentation. Given this, make sure you have built time into the schedule to accommodate questions and answers.

- **The main message**: Keep in mind that people in the audience have a limited capacity to retain information. So reduce what you have to a few key points and remind the audience often what they are. State them in the introduction, flesh them out in the body of the presentation, and repeat them again in summary form to close. If you have a lot of good material, it will make very little difference if you forget to mention something you had planned to say. After all, the audience doesn't know if you have left out something. In client presentations, you may find that some part of your report will be of great interest—so much so that you will want to pursue it with them at the risk of cutting the rest of your presentation short; in these situations, it is helpful to let them know that this might be the case. With client presentations, be prepared for diversions and accommodate to them accordingly.

- **Closing**: It can be motivational, challenging, thoughtful, and, without exception, a restatement of your main points. With a client group it may be a restatement of the next steps to be taken to move the consultation to the next phase of implementation. For general audiences, this ending segment will have a strong influence on what they take home with them when the presentation is over.

> *Tell them the truth, first because it's the right thing to do and second—they'll find out anyway.*
>
> Paul Galvin

The Art of Giving Client Feedback and Surviving to Consult Again

Of all the communication skills that are central to the consultant's success, giving feedback to clients may be the most difficult and the most important. While *giving and receiving feedback* was mentioned earlier in the discussion of interpersonal skills in general, we want to tie it more directly to feedback as a crucial consulting responsibility.

All too often the value and appropriateness of feedback depends on whether or not the recipient is prepared to hear it. There are a number of things you can do to help your client be receptive to feedback. But first we will look at the types of feedback situations that are closely associated with the work of a consultant.

- **Feedback of data from a survey or from a series of interviews**: This kind of feedback is often associated with the consultant's data gathering responsibilities. The client needs to know the results of the survey or interviews before making some critical decisions. Not all the information is positive and the consultant knows the client doesn't take bad news lightly. The feedback session could be fraught with controversy. What to do?

- **Feedback to a group that specifically has requested a consultant to interview its members**: The intent might be to learn their individual feelings and reactions about the way the group is going about its work and then report back *to the group as a whole*. It is a good way to help the group generate crucial data that might be hampering its overall effectiveness without singling out anyone in particular. For this kind of feedback to be effective, the consultant role is to help the group understand what the data says and gain acceptance of it so there is some hope that remedial action, if needed, will be undertaken.

- **Feedback to individuals**: This is appropriate when some data has been gathered about the individual either from direct observation or interviews and the individual has indicated a willingness to hear the feedback. In order for the feedback to be effective, the consultant must ask the right questions, observe the behavior concerned, and give the feedback in a manner that will facilitate learning. In other words, the feedback must be concrete, descriptive, verifiable, timely, and specific.

The following are some generally accepted rules of engagement about giving and receiving feedback:

- **Focus feedback on behavior rather than the person**. It is important to focus the feedback on what a person *does* rather than comment on what we imagine he *is*. It is less threatening to an individual to hear about his behavior than his traits. This strategy also implies something specific that can be changed.

- **Focus feedback on observations rather than inferences.** Observations are what we actually see while inferences are conclusions drawn from these observations.

- **Focus feedback on description rather than judgment.** The effort to describe is a process of reporting while judgment suggests a good or bad, right or wrong evaluation. Description is value neutral; judgment arises out of our personal frames of reference.

- **Focus feedback on specific "here and now" situations rather than abstract behavior.** Feedback is more meaningful to the person receiving it when it comes as soon as possible after the observed behavior actually occurs.

- **Focus feedback on the sharing of ideas and information rather than on advice giving.** Sharing ideas and information leaves the recipient free to choose what to do in light of her own goals at the time and in the situation. By offering advice or by telling someone what to do, the freedom choice is taken away.

- **Focus feedback on exploring alternatives rather than answers or solutions.** The more the focus on different means for attaining a goal, the less likely we are to accept a premature solution.

- **Focus feedback on the amount of information the person can use rather than the amount available to be given.** To overload a person with feedback is to reduce the possibility that she will effectively the information she receives.

- **Focus feedback on time and place.** Many emotional reactions and feelings can be associated with feedback. It is important to be sensitive to the appropriate time for giving it to avoid doing more harm than good.

Good counselors lack no clients.

William Shakespeare

V. The Client Relationship Challenge

***

What you can expect to find in this chapter:

- Key concerns that affect consultant-client relationships
- Strategies for building your business
- The role of research and assessment in consulting
- Consultant initiated proposals
- RFPs, contracts, and other potential distractions
- Ethics and consulting
- Defining success: as a client, as a consultant

Developing and maintaining productive and positive consultant-client relationships is the most important and often the most difficult challenge for consultants. The difficulty results from the need to work at several levels of interaction at once. First of all, there is the task-oriented focus of the relationship, the rational and explicit reasons that bring consultants and clients together. Secondly, there is what we might describe as the *affective* or feeling levels of interaction between the two parties. Most consulting involves close collaboration by individuals who represent different institutional settings and mindsets. Finally, there are the norms and values that define their separate worlds of engagement.

Key issues and concerns that affect client-consultant relationships

Let's look at some of the more important issues and concerns that can affect your consulting relationships with clients.

- Is there an understanding that the responsibilities for success—
  and failure—are equally shared between you and your client?
  There is a tendency for consultants and clients to blame each
  other when the relationship and the intended results of the
  collaborative initiative go awry.

- Can the relationship be built and maintained on mutual
  honesty and truthfulness? Telling the other party what you
  think they want to hear, rather than the truth, is an unfortunate
  legacy of many consulting-client relationships.

- Are the feelings of all the parties to the consultation seen as
  legitimate concerns that can be discussed in a direct and caring
  way? Consulting-client relationships often falter on issues of
  control, breakdowns in communication, abdication of responsibilities, and many more dysfunctional behaviors. Unless there
  is an explicit understanding that these behaviors can be discussed safely, they can spiral into anger, hostility, and mistrust.

- Do the parties to the collaborative relationship trust each other?
  In operational terms trust is about honoring confidentiality, not
  undermining each other's involvement or credibility, communicating openly about concerns, and more.

- Is there a clear understanding and agreement about those
  aspects of the relationship that might have ethical consequences?

Consultancies are interventions. Interventions are actions taken by
outsiders to help insiders function more effectively and efficiently. For
interventions to be successful, they must be able to generate useful and
valid information, help those in the client system make free and open
choices, and develop internal commitment to follow through on the
planned outcomes. All three of these criteria are integral to the capacity
building norms and values associated with process consulting.

Before the consultant and client arrive at the point where they can
talk about these criteria, Alan Weiss says the consultant and client
normally will go through a series of small but progressive steps in their
relationship. In other words, contracts don't normally fall like ripe fruit
into the consultant's lap on the first encounter. Weiss describes the
progression as often involving the following steps, after which a "yes"
on the part of both parties is needed before they continue.

- The progression starts out with the initial contact between the consultant and client, one that could have been initiated by the consultant based on a lead, referral, or a lucky encounter. They exchange acknowledgments, provide a bit of background, and agree to meet again.

- The second contact may involve the exchange of information or materials leading to an agreement to hold a brief meeting.

- A brief meeting is held to form a working relationship and to agree on a second more substantive meeting.

- The second meeting results in a conceptual agreement about the nature of the consultancy and the client's willingness to entertain a proposal.

- The proposal is drafted, discussed, and revised. If acceptable to each party, the project is initiated. (2000, p.134)

While this sounds very time-consuming and ritualistic, developing satisfactory long-term, client-consulting relationships is akin to mating dance rituals. While the ritual may vary from culture to culture, it is a process that each consultant needs to appreciate and understand.

Once you and your client have agreed to work together, you need to:

- **Reach a mutual understanding about the focus of the consultancy.** While this understanding might shift as you enter into the information gathering and analysis process, you and your client need to agree on the starting definition for the proposed intervention.

- **Explore what each party brings to, and wants from, the intervention.** These often are referred to as each side's "wants and offers," or your mutual expectations about how you will work together.

- **Agree on some fundamental operating principles.** These include specific objectives to be pursued; the need for and access to pertinent information needed to conduct the consultancy; recognition of potential time constraints and other botherations that can thwart initiatives on both sides; and clarity about the expected outputs and outcomes of the consultancy.

If these discussions go well, the consultant and client should be able to agree on compensation and other monetary-type details. This all sounds very complex and lengthy, but buying the services as a consultant is not like buying something off the shelf of your local super market. (To learn more about how to establish an effective relationship with your client, check out the Toolkit section of this Guide.)

Business Development Strategies

Building a successful consulting business is first of all hard work. It also requires you to pursue a number of different strategies simultaneously unless, of course, you are blessed with an unusual amount of luck and charm. Here are a few of the more common strategies to consider.

- Take the initiative in developing your own proposals to prospective clients. These actions often result from the types of interactive dialogues that have just been discussed. The client likes what she has learned in an interaction with you and asks for a proposal.

- Once you have developed a working relationship with a client, help that client understand and appreciate ways to expand your involvement in his enterprise. If, for example, you facilitate the development of a strategic plan by the management team, help them understand how you can help to implement and evaluate specific components of the plan.

- Never hesitate to ask your client for references. These fall roughly into two categories: 1) the usual letter of reference or a well-placed phone call on your behalf to praise your attributes and 2) other individuals or enterprises you should contact to carry out similar consulting initiatives. The second kind is usually more immediate and productive.

- Respond to formal requests for proposals (RFPs) from various sources. These are usually competitive bidding arrangements based on scopes of work and criteria that are developed by the client. Based on this approach, you would probably be competing against many other consultants so the odds of getting the contract are greatly reduced.

- Conduct surveys or assessments that result in an information or data base that is of interest to prospective clients. Often these surveys or assessments are an integral part of some consulting assignment. At other times, the survey or assessment is external to a specific client but of interest to the client for one reason or another.

Given the importance of these business development strategies, let's look at some of the more significant ones in-depth.

The Fine Art of Research and Assessment

While it sounds terribly academic, successful consultants engage in a variety of survey and assessment techniques with current and prospective clients. The rationale for these activities includes developing a reliable information and data bank to support your initial intervention with the client and using that intervention to justify the need for future interventions. Here are a couple of examples of how this works.

- **Example # 1**: You are hired to conduct a training needs assessment for the marketing department of a rapidly expanding enterprise. Taking a performance discrepancy approach to the assessment, you identify performance problems that require non-training responses. In addition to being contracted to provide training, based on the results of the assessment, you also are asked to provide non-training related consulting support.

- **Example # 2**: You are a member of a small team of performance budgeting specialists who have been hired to help the finance department of a small manufacturing company work with operating departments to develop ISO performance indicators and benchmarks. In your work with the finance department, you conduct a survey of the operating departments to identify implementation concerns. While most departments are willing to implement the new system, they uniformly complained that they don't have the staff resources to carry out the program effectively. Based on this information, the chief executive officer asks you and your team to work with the human resource management department to conduct a staffing review of the organization.

In each of these examples, the value-added contract for your services resulted from an assessment of the client's needs resulting from the initial contract. While it is easier and less expensive to gain more work from an existing client than to find new ones, you will also need to pursue new opportunities. Here are some thoughts on how to do this.

Using surveys and assessments to find new clients

Some consultants conduct surveys and assessments to identify new consulting opportunities and find new markets, based on the resulting data and information. Often these surveys are conducted in conjunction with professional associations or membership and educational organizations.

- **Example # 1:** You have convinced a local government association that it is in the best interest of its members to know the extent to which local governments are involving citizens in the budgeting process. You've also suggested that they may want to document some of the best participatory budgeting practices. As a result of your suggestion, you are hired to help the association design and conduct the survey. As their consultant on this survey, you gain the inside track on follow-up business. You might, for example, also be hired by the association to conduct workshops around the country on the results of the survey. In addition, individual cities may hire you to help them develop a more citizen-friendly budgeting process.

- **Example #2:** Like many enterprising consultants, you are teaching a management course at the local university. In a conversation with the Dean, you learn that she is interested in learning more about the market demand for graduates in retail management. You indicate to her that you would be interested in conducting a survey of large retail organizations to assess their need for such specialized graduates. In your assessment you learn that many retailers are interested but want the university to consider initiating a formal internship program as part of the curriculum. This would provide them an opportunity to assess the potential of future employees before hiring them full-time. Since you have good relations with many of these retail organizations, the university asks you to manage the intern program.

These examples illustrate the kinds of indirect marketing strategies you can use to build your business. Successful consulting entrepreneurs rarely draw tight boundaries around their competencies as a consultant or around their clientele systems. Surveys and assessments, whether initiated by the consultant or conducted for clients, can be fertile ground for new consulting opportunities.

Conducting surveys and assessments can be relatively simple—or very complex. The process can involve a small number of individuals, such as members of a senior management team, to all the directors of a country-wide network of downtown business associations. Surveys and assessments can be qualitative or quantitative, structured or exploratory, proactive or reactive. Regardless of their context or scope, surveys and assessment have one thing in common: They are designed to produce additional information, data, insights, and impressions about whatever they are focused on. They also can be one of your best strategies for expanding your consulting opportunities with current clients—and for developing new clients. Check out the Toolkit for more ideas on how to design and conduct successful surveys and assessments.

Developing Consultant-Initiated Proposals

Like business plans, there seems to be no universal template for developing a non-solicited business proposal. Nevertheless, there are certain guidelines to consider if you decide to become a proactive proposal writer. For example:

- How you initiate the proposal is important. Proposals that evolve out of verbal interactions between the client and the consultant have a much better chance of being accepted and, in the long run, implemented successfully. Unannounced, unsolicited proposals are, more often than not, candidates for the waste bin.

- Collect as much information as you can about the situation. Better to have too much information than not enough.

- Proposals that leave room for incremental inputs from the consultant and the client's representatives who will be involved in implementation demonstrate mutual trust and a commitment to on-the-job learning.

- To the extent possible, the proposal should describe briefly the outputs and outcomes of the proposed intervention. Outputs are the immediate benefits expected from the intervention. Outcomes are the longer-term consequences of a successful intervention.

- Milestones of progress should be identified, if possible, along with performance criteria.

- Identify, as much as you can, those who will be accountable for inputs and actions throughout the intervention.

- Describe the process you plan to use in conducting the consultancy.

- If there are to be options available to the client as the project advances, these should be noted in the proposal.

- Include some details on how you typically bill for your services and what your fees are. Most managers will want to figure out the bottom line to your unsolicited opportunity to help them.

- Finally, recognize that negotiation is an acceptable process for clarifying any and all parts of any proposed program, project, or intervention strategy.

Suggested proposal outline

The following is a suggested outline for writing credible and hopefully winning proposals. Modify it to meet your needs, local norms, and conditions. The term *intervention* has been used as a generic term for identifying the intended project or program. If this sounds too clinical, change it.

1. Cover letter: helps the client know whom to contact and how. It's also important to let the client know when and how you will be following up on the proposal. Otherwise, it could end up feeding the office shredder.

2. Executive summary: saying what you said in the proposal but in one page.

3. Description of the situation that prompted the proposal: the **why** of the proposed intervention. Hopefully, this is a mutually agreed upon definition of the situation and the urgency for action.

4. Objectives and measurement criteria: **what** you hope to achieve as a result of the proposed intervention and how success will be determined. The impact assessment begins with writing clear and unambiguous objectives.

5. Methodology and description of activities to be undertaken: the **how** of the proposed intervention. If this is a process consultancy, it will be important to describe briefly the interactive nature of the proposed project or program. Also consider any options that might have been discussed that would be considered during the life of the intervention.

6. Potential challenges and conditions that may affect the quality of the work to be done. If there are potential problems that seem obvious from the beginning, it may be important to address them in the proposal.

7. Timetable of key activities, including the beginning and expected completion: the **when** which is tied closely to the details in Step 5.

8. Roles and responsibilities of key participants. This is the all important **who will do what with whom.** Don't forget to include your own qualifications and tailor them to the proposed intervention.

9. The terms and conditions of payments: fees, reimbursable expenses, and any other financial arrangements that need to be considered.

10. A final sign-off statement that indicates the proposal's acceptance by both parties.

While most of these steps aren't sacred, they are important.

RFPs, Contracts, and Other Potential Distractions

RFPs: Requests for Proposal. The previous section assumes that proposals are, more often than not, consultant-initiated. Most successful proposals emerge out of client-consultant conversations where the client may even ask for a proposal based on the discussions. In most cases, these proposals are not competitive. The client wants your ideas and is willing to work with you on developing the proposal.

Requests for proposals, as the term suggests, are client-initiated. More often than not, they are competitive, although those eligible to bid may be limited in many cases by pre-bid qualifications. This allows the initiator of the process to manage the response. Most governments operate through the RFP process unless the amount of the project or program being bid is limited in scope and value.

Organizations use the RFP process for several reasons:

- All qualified bidders are aware of the opportunity to place a bid.

- The evaluation of bids is easier since everyone is bidding against the same criteria.

- Presumably the best price is obtained.

Most individual consultants prefer not to pursue RFPs for the following reasons:

- Most requests for proposals require the services of organizations with significant human resources at their command.

- Even if an individual consultant might be able to assemble a consortium of resources, responding to formal RFPs can be time-consuming and expensive.

- The bid documents are often complicated and require specialized help in responding according to the bid specifications.

- The competition can be fierce, thus diminishing the potential for winning the award.

- The odds of winning are not worth the effort that goes into the preparation.

In spite of these odds, there are some situations where it might be advisable to respond to a request for proposal:

- You might have special skills or experience that few other consultants have and the organization has targeted you as one of a few who is qualified.

- You are experiencing a lull in your work schedule and decide to send in a proposal although you know the odds of winning might be minimal.

- You want the experience of competing with your competition.

- The value of the proposed project is too enticing to ignore and you are willing to compete for it.

- You're bored and have nothing better to do.

Chasing RFPs is not a good way for a new consulting business to spend its time.

Contracts. Formal contracts will be dictated, in large measure, by local regulations and traditions. Given this, it makes little sense to detail here what they might include. What does make sense is sharing some of the most valuable insights and advice available regarding consultants and contracts. Alan Weiss, in *Getting Started in Consulting*, says that proposals, discussed earlier, shouldn't be turned into legal contracts with boilerplate language, such as "parties of the third part" or other legalese. He provides several key reasons to keep proposals conversational and not legal:

- Consulting is a business built on mutual trust. Inserting legal language into your proposal immediately summons the client's lawyers and purchasing agents. Delays may be the least of your worries when they get hold of your proposal.

- The notion that a lone consultant may find protection through a legal contract is, in Weiss's words, "silly." You no doubt will be dealing with clients who have many more resources to contest anything written on paper. (2000, pp. 139-40) Weiss counsels consultants to: 1) engage in conversations with their clients to reach mutual agreement on the conceptual framework of their work together and 2) provide a quick follow-up proposal in writing that is clear, concise, and covers all the essentials for assuring a productive working relationship.

Keep your client relations simple. Satisfied clients are the consultant's best friends. They help you find more business within their own companies, and they refer you to their friends and other business associates. Consulting is a business built largely on relationships that are, in turn, built on trust. Trust is earned through hard work, competent services, and integrity. Anything that complicates these relationships will cost you time and, consequently, money.

Ethics and Consulting

There is no more important issue in building and sustaining a consulting business than ethics. Your ethical behavior will define not just the quality of your work but your reputation as a professional. Given the importance of ethics, it is a fitting way to conclude this section on consultant-client relationship challenges.

Ethics is a two-way responsibility. Ethical behavior is at the heart of the consulting process. If *trust* is the core value upon which effective consulting relationships are established, then a practiced code of ethics is the fuel that sustains it. Both the consultant and client need to adhere to ethical standards that are understood by both parties.

From the consultant's perspective, your code of ethics should cover these virtues:

- *Confidentiality* both within the organization where the consulting is taking place and beyond. To be effective, consultants need to hear many different perspectives about what is going on within the context of the consultancy. Only through assurance of confidentiality will this happen. That confidentiality must be honored. It goes without saying that consultants must also protect that confidentiality beyond the boundaries of the client organization.

- *Honesty* about billing rates, expenses, credentials and capability, timekeeping, and, most importantly, when giving advice and recommendations.

- *Honoring intellectual properties* by giving proper credit for the work of others.

At the same time, avoid these ethical pitfalls:

- *Conflicts of interest,* including consulting with two organizations that are in direct competition with each other or making recommendations that will benefit other interests that you might represent. At a minimum, disclose them openly. Better yet, don't get involved in them.

- *Engaging in data gathering shenanigans,* such as making the information up, skewing it to fit your point of view or recommendations, or selling it to your client's competitors.

- *Using your client's organization as a recruiting ground for your own organization or other clients.*

- _____(add other principles and practices that you believe need to be included in a consultant's code of ethics)

From your clients, you should expect the following principles to be honored in your business relationships with them:

- *Honesty* in the objectives they want to achieve with your help, in establishing contacts for information gathering, and when using the results of your collaborative efforts.

- *Respect your confidentiality* by not insisting, for example, that you tell everything you learned from employees and other parties while researching the situation.

- *Appreciation for your time and other needs,* such as getting paid fairly and punctually for the work you have done.

- *Understanding and respecting your code of ethics* by not asking you to do things that would be in violation of your principles.

- _____(with experience, come back and add more)

Since consulting is largely about forging honest and trusting relationships between parties with differing needs and expectations, it is critical that both sides discuss the principles of engagement upon which they want their relationship to be built. The initial contracting stage is the time to clarify any concerns you might have about operating within your personal code of ethics.

The secret of success is constancy to purpose.

Benjamin Disraeli

Defining Success from the Client's Perspective

At the heart of every consultant-client relationship is the need for success. Sustaining a successful consulting business will depend, in large measure, on how your clients judge your relationship with them and other key stakeholders in the intervention as well as the quality of your products, advice, and services. Here are some questions that both you and the client should be thinking about as you conduct your business together.

- Was the quality of your work more than satisfactory? "Just satisfactory" isn't enough to build a business!

- Did you do what you said you would do?

- Did you meet deadlines and other criteria established at the beginning of the relationship?

- Were your costs in line with your competition and the value of the services given?

- Did you maintain effective means of communication throughout the consultancy?

- Did you honor the client's needs for confidentiality?

- Were you honest in your relationships and in your recommendations?

- Did you avoid conflicts of interest within the organization and beyond?

- Were you flexible and adaptive to new situations as they evolved during the consultancy?

- Did you demonstrate the ability to "think outside the box"—to be creative in your approach to challenges and recommendations?

- Were you dependable?

- Were you fair and inclusive in your relationships with all those with whom you interacted during the consultancy?

- Did you use your time, and your client's time, efficiently and effectively?

For the client, the most important question is: Would you employ this consultant again?

For the consultant, there are several questions:

- What have you learned from this consultancy?

- What will you do differently in your next consulting assignment, based on what you have learned?

- Would you take another contract from this client?

Defining Success from Your Perspective As a Consultant

While your success as a consultant will depend in large measure on the views of your clients, you also should be looking in the mirror to assess your success as you see it. The following questionnaire is designed to help you engage in a bit of self-assessment and reflection. There are two parts: The first is determining how successful you think you have been from the client's perspective. This requires you to step into the client's shoes in order to make the judgment. The second is more personal but no less important.

Each statement is followed by a space to record the percentage of times you think your consulting meets the criteria. For example, you might assess the quality of your work as being *more than satisfactory* 70% of the time. We believe this self-assessment can help you focus on specific aspects of your consulting experiences that can be improved to further your career as a consultant.

Client Related Success Criteria:

1. The overall quality of my consulting work is **more than satisfactory.** ____%

2. I do what I say I will do in working with my clients. ____%

3. I meet deadlines and other criteria agreed upon with my clients. ____%

4. My costs are in line with my competition. ____%

5. The value of my services meets my clients' expectations. ____%

6. I maintain effective means of communication with my clients. ____%

7. I respect and honor my client's needs for confidentiality. ____%

8. I'm honest in my client relationships and recommendations. ____%

9. I avoid conflicts of interest within the clients' organizations and beyond. ____%

10. I'm flexible and adaptive to new situations in my work with clients. ____%

11. I am creative in my approach to challenges and recommendations. ____%

12. I am dependable. ____%

Personal Success Criteria:

1. I am satisfied with my decision to become a consultant. ____%

2. I enjoy my work as a consultant. ____%

3. My financial rewards from consulting meet my expectations. ____%

4. I can live with the consequences of not having a steady, reliable income. ____%

5. I have been able to set aside money for unexpected problems, i.e. sickness. ____%

6. I spend enough time on my family and other non-work respon-sibilities. ____%

7. The time I spend away from home consulting is not a problem. ____%

8. I allocate time and resources for my professional development. ___%

9. I am able to manage my time effectively as a consultant. ____%

10. I have no regrets about my decision to become a consultant. ____%

Don't hesitate to add additional criteria to either or both of these categories.

Add up your scores in each category and divide them by the number of criteria in each category.

My average score in client oriented success is____%
My average score in my personal success criteria is ___%

Only you can decide if these scores meet your personal expecta-tions. Nevertheless, if any of the individual scores are less than 80%, you might want to develop a strategy for increasing the score. After all, the profession of consulting is based on setting and achieving high standards in working with your clients. It is, in fact, the only way to build and maintain a successful business. You should not accept low standards on any of the criteria that affect your personal lifestyle as a consultant. Both sides of this lifestyle commitment are important.

And remember: Success as a consultant is not the result of sponta-neous combustion. You must set yourself on fire and continue to fan the flames if you want to be successful.

*Every tool carries with it the spirit by which it
has been created.*

Werner Karl Heisenberg

VI. A Few Basic Tools to Add to Your Survival Kit

What you can expect to find in this chapter:

- Some thoughts on how to manage your time
- Collaboration: the second commandment of consulting
- The art of successful client contracting
- Problems and opportunities: welcome to the bi-polar world of client-centered consulting
- Action research and participatory planning
- Various ways to collect information and data
- Strategic planning, visioning, and other forward looking stuff
- Staff development and training interventions

The tools that follow are organized roughly by types of intervention. By "intervention" we mean any deliberate act, influence, or activity on the part of the consultant that brings about change. Interventions happen at various levels of engagement and intensity. For example, the first two tools we offer are designed to help you intervene into your own life space to bring about changes in your thought patterns and behavior. Time management is mostly about how you behave as a consultant in relation to a finite resource you have at your disposal—TIME! The second tool also can be used for personal introspection or as a means to help overcome resistance on the part of a perspective client.

From these more personal tools we move to those that deal primarily with one-on-one interventions, i.e. the client-consultant contracting dialogue and the art of holding skillful discussions. Progressing right along, we move to team-oriented tools such as strategic planning and associated intervention activities, i.e. stakeholder analysis. Finally, we will share a few preferred tools for conducting organization or larger systems interventions. These include action research and training and development interventions.

As we progress from the more personal types of interventions to those more likely associated with larger systems, we urge you not to be as dogmatic as we might sound in trying to shoehorn these tools into specific categories. Use them if, when, and where you believe they might fit to help you be more effective in your intervention activities.

Tooling right along, here are some of our favorite tools of the consulting trade.

Tool 1: Managing Your Time

Your most valuable asset as a consultant is time. It's how you normally bill your services. If you spend your time on things that can't be billed to someone else, it takes money out of your pocket. The problem with time is that it's finite. Unlike other resources, time can't be replaced. You spend it today, it's gone. The best opportunity you have to conserve your time—so you can have someone else pay for it—is to *manage* it.

Typical time wasters include lack of planning, handling the same work more than once, desk clutter, failing to assign routine work to others capable of doing it, allowing visitor and telephone interruptions, too many meetings, procrastination, and indecision. Among the most effective ways to overcome these time wasters is to manage your time. Time management specialists agree that the following eight personal habits are among the most effective ways to manage your time.

1. **Focus on what is most important**. Set aside time each day or week to think about and to work on what matters most in your life. When you pay enough attention to the most important things, you will significantly diminish the number of urgent issues, particularly the number of crises.

2. **Consolidate your time**. Set aside large blocks of time, 45 to 90 minutes at a time, during which you concentrate on one important thing until it is finished or you are satisfied with the progress that has been made.

3. **Recognize your limits**. Sometimes the flow of ideas simply dries up. Rather than sitting there in angry frustration, find

something less demanding and routine to do to make use of the time until the ideas begin to flow again.

4. **Follow your internal clock.** Some people do their best work early in the day; others do better at day's end. Recognize your own best time of day for productive work and use this time to work on priority items.

5. **Get organized.** Organize what you have to do in a way that makes sense to you. Some people like a neat desk. Others get creative energy with piles of material in plain sight. Any system that enables you to find what you need quickly without a long, frustrating search is a good system.

6. **Subdivide overwhelming tasks.** Break big tasks into smaller pieces that can be completed with relative ease. Large projects are often put off, day after day, because the prospect of getting started on them is so intimidating.

7. **Keep track of commitments.** A good way to start or end the day is to update a running list of the important things that need to be done in the next few days. If an item remains on the list for long without serious consequences to you or others, consider dropping it from the list altogether.

8. **Just say "no."** This is the most important way to prevent unscheduled or unwanted activities to intrude on accomplishing the things that matter most. Consider the time consequences, eventual payoffs, and opportunity cost of every new thing with a time dimension that comes across your desk.

Michael LeBoeuf claims that most of us waste half our time, and most wasted time is due to poor habits and lack of self-discipline. He says it takes about three weeks to convert a new way of doing things into a comfortable habit. If you are not using any of the preceding time saving techniques and want to start, LeBoeuf suggests choosing just one of them, doing it for three weeks, and giving yourself a reward for doing it successfully. He also suggests deciding on the reward before you start so that it will serve as motivation for you to stay the course. (1989, p.7) Time management isn't easy but it's important. Time, after all, is your most valuable asset as a consultant.

Tool 2: Dealing With Resistance

Consultants inevitably will encounter resistance in their efforts to build a consulting business. This resistance sometimes is self-imposed. This is why we suggested earlier that you might encounter resistance in your own behavior. That resistance can come early, as you engage in marketing, as well as later, when you become involved in helping bring about changes in work settings. There is a tendency to believe that resistance can be overcome if we can assemble the right set of data or compose the most persuasive argument. Unfortunately, this confrontational strategy demonstrates a major misunderstanding of the nature of resistance.

Resistance is, more often than not, an emotional response. In his analysis of the consultant's role in dealing with resistance, Peter Block argues that resistance is an emotional process. Because it is emotional and not rational, he contends there is no way you can talk a client out of her resistance. If you meet the resistance head on, in an attempt to conquer it, you only will intensify the storm.

The alternative Block proposes for helping the client get beyond the resistance so she can concentrate on solving the problem has a Zen-like quality to it. The strategy is to help the storm gradually "blow itself out." He suggests a simple, three-step approach for overcoming resistance:

Step 1. Identify what form the resistance is taking based on non-verbal messages from the client, such as constantly moving away, pointing fingers, clenching fists, or nodding her head from side to side when you speak. There may be verbal clues as well. The client may express frustration and feelings of being misunderstood: "Let me explain something to you…" Then, compose in your head, not out loud, some words of your own to describe what you see the client doing or saying.

Step 2. State, in a neutral, non-punishing way, the form the resistance is taking. This is called "naming the resistance." The trick is to find neutral, everyday language to describe the resistance. For example, if the consultant sees the resistance as an attack on himself, a possible response might be: "You are questioning a lot of what I do. You seem angry about something."

Step 3. Be quiet and let the client respond to your statement about the resistance "until the storm passes." (Block, pp. 131-6)

As we can see, resistance is not terribly responsive to counter-resistance. Kurt Lewin, one of our great silent mentors in this business, gave us one of the most important problem solving tools ever invented: force field analysis. It's both simple and profound. Every force creates a counterforce which helps to keep things in equilibrium. To change the status quo, Lewin counsels us to resist putting more pressure on the driving force and to deal with the restraining force or forces. In other words, deal with the resistance. By the way, you will find our version of the force field analysis tool later on.

Tool 3: Collaboration— The Second Commandment of Consulting

"What is the first?" you ask. Communication, of course. And, the art of effective communication with your client must necessarily be wrapped around the need and the will to collaborate in order to achieve your client's goals. A consultancy usually begins when someone in an organization (the client) discovers that something isn't right and decides that someone from outside the organization (the consultant) is needed to help set it right. In other words, they decide to collaborate.

In this collaboration, the consultant's task is to verify the client's perception of the problem and either: 1) tell the client what to do about it, based on the consultant's technical expertise, or 2) collaborate with the client in reaching a solution. Consulting authority Peter Block believes there are two reasons why consultants strive for collaborative relationships with their clients.

1. Collaboration makes the best possible use of available resources, the consultant's and the client's, while spreading out the responsibility for success and implementation. The consultant is in no position to order the client to do anything. So, ownership of a consultant's proposals must be shifted to the client, step-by-step, during the consulting process. Building client ownership is often a matter of removing obstacles that might hinder implementation of the consultant's proposals.

2. Collaboration allows the consultant, whether intentionally or not, to give the client a working model of how problems are solved. The consultant's goal is to help the client solve problems so they stay solved. Through collaboration, the client

develops a problem solving capacity that may not have existed before. The next time a problem arises, the client will have the skills to solve it without reliance on outside help. (1981, pp. 16-23)

3. Collaborations are not self-sustaining. They need nurturing and a lot of hard work to withstand the inevitable strains of pursuing common interests. The National Civic League, widely regarded for its initiatives in supporting collaborative ventures at the local governance level, offers these guidelines.

4. For collaborative initiatives to be successful they require:

   - Good timing and a sense of urgency about working together.

   - Broad-based involvement from all parties involved in the intervention.

   - A process of shared decision making that is seen as fair and open to everyone with an interest.

   - Commitment and/or involvement of top management.

   - The establishment of mutual trust early in the process.

   - Leadership to work through difficulties and acknowledge successes.

   - Recognition and celebration of interim successes. (1994, pp. 51-4)

In addition to these important elements, those involved in collaborative initiatives must be able to communicate clearly and convincingly with each other.

Tool 4: The Art of Client-Consultant Contracting

Collaboration begins with the contracting process. Once the consultant and client have decided to work together, they need to enter into the "contracting" phase of the relationship. The contracting process includes two distinct components.

1. **The formal agreement about working together.** This covers details like how much time will be devoted to the consultation, the services to be performed, and how compensation for the consultant's services will be handled. These details might be in the consultant's proposal or could be embodied in a letter of agreement. Reaching a formal agreement is more directly associated with managing and building a consulting business. The details on how to handle this part of the contracting process can be found in Part One of this Guide.

2. **The more personal agreement about how to work together.** This deals with relationship issues and concerns, or, how to collaborate in decision making and problem solving. While it is often called the social or psychological contract, it could just as easily be referred to as the *operational contract*. While it is associated with the initial stages of consultant—client collaboration, it sets the conditions and tone of the entire consultancy. Because it is such an important part of initiating the consulting process with the client, it is important to know what it entails.

Peter Block, in *Flawless Consulting*, provides one of the clearest interpretations of what needs to be covered in this initial contracting meeting between a consultant and a client. His approach includes the following five steps.

- *Personal Acknowledgment.* The consultant can take advantage of this first contact to express her feelings about the consulting opportunity and to learn how and why the client decided to initiate the contact.

- *Communicating and Understanding the Situation.* This is the consultant's opportunity to ask questions about the client's perspective on the situation and to convey his understanding of what is involved.

- *Client Wants and Offers.* It is at this point that the consultant raises questions to gain a clear understanding of the client's expectations for the work relationship.

- *Consultant Wants and Needs.* Before ending the meeting, the consultant will want to state her expectations for the relationship and what must happen for the venture to be a success. The consultant may also need clarification about the consulting role the client has in mind. It is important for the consultant to be forthright and assertive about her wants and needs at this stage of contracting. This is necessary to avoid role disagreements later when the stakes are higher.

- *Resolving Remaining Issues and Concerns.* After the foregoing matters have been discussed thoroughly, the consultant might restate the key issues and strive to resolve any remaining concerns. For example, the client may have lingering concerns about losing control as the consultant works with others in the organization. These concerns must be resolved before a mutual commitment is made to move ahead. A final step might be giving the client positive support for the initiatives to be taken and to be clear about what happens next. (1981, pp. 55-85)

Out of this phase of the contracting process should emerge the following information and agreements on how the consultancy will be conducted.

- *What are the objectives of the proposed intervention?* The more precisely this is stated, the more likely the success of the relationship.

- *What are the parameters of the project?* It is important to draw boundaries around the project that show clearly what work is included and what work is excluded.

- *What kind of information will be needed?* Date requirements and access to information, including the time it will take to collect it, are matters to be addressed.

- *What kind of support will be needed by the client and the consultant?* These might include meeting space, equipment, and staff time.

- *What are the time constraints?* This is important since the client may have one deadline in mind and the consultant another.

- *What outputs are expected to be delivered?* Will they include a training workshop, problem solving sessions, a final report? Don't forget that the process itself can be a deliverable if you are engaged in *process consultation.*

- *What values need to be made explicit and upheld?* This may be more difficult to define. While the need for adherence to a set of ground rules for meetings may not be difficult, the openness with which a consultant's output is shared may be sensitive for personal or political reasons.

Once these issues are clarified and agreed upon by both the consultant and client, the consultancy can begin in earnest. If this stage in the collaborative process is not pursued, the consultancy can be jeopardized by miscommunication and misunderstanding later on. This is not to suggest that the issues and concerns, covered in Peter Block's five step approach to building the relationship, will not reoccur for more discussion as the consultancy unfolds. Nevertheless, they provide the initial understanding that can be revisited, if and when the psychological contract needs revision.

Before moving on to the more generic skills and tools that consultants need to be effective in providing their services, it is important to address one more important aspect of both the initial phases of psychological and operational contracting as well as the on-going process of collaboration: how to deal with resistance to your ideas, your methods, and your presence.

Tool 5: Understanding Your Client's Bipolar Personality

Before delving too deeply into this bag of consulting skills, it will be helpful to stop for a moment and look at the client's perceived need for your services. One of the few certainties in the life of individuals and organizations is change. Most changes either result in *problems* the client needs to solve or *opportunities* the client can exploit. Problems, more often than not, are associated with client *awareness* that something is wrong and needs fixing. Opportunities are often less noticeable and evolve out of the client's *vision* of a better future. The processes used to deal with these phenomena are quite different. These differences are important for consultants to keep in mind as they interact with their clients.

- *Problems* are related to the past. They are considered undesirable and potentially harmful—the result of what was done or not done before. Understanding them requires hindsight in order to discover what went wrong and as the basis for corrective action. Ignoring them could be a serious mistake, leading to more serious consequences over time.

- *Opportunities* are related to the future. They are viewed as desirable and potentially beneficial, usually based on theories or the experience of others. Rather than being understood, they must be imagined through foresight and visions of what might be. Unlike problems, they can be ignored although doing so could be a source of significant future regret.

Here are six common examples of *problems* and *opportunities*. You decide which is which.

- *New leadership.* In response to a significant turnover of governing body officials, an organization must move quickly to achieve a shared sense of direction, order, and continuity.

- *New organization.* A recently created organization has selected its management and operating staff and they are under pressure to clarify their future role to key constituents.

- *Financial crisis.* The loss of an important income source has resulted in a cutback in professional staff, prompting the need to rethink types and levels of service to be delivered.

- *Expanded role.* A national redefinition of functional assignments has expanded the organization's role to include new services and new clients.

- *Inertia.* An organization suffering from ineffective management and a general decline in service quality is threatened with closure if it doesn't make significant changes.

- *Merger.* An organization is under political pressure to merge with another organization without being given time and resources to plan the changes.

Problems and opportunities are the consultant's friends. Without them, consultants would be doing something else to earn a living. How you approach them is important. Sometimes problems can also be opportunities for the client, and opportunities can be problematic. Your role is to help the client make the most of every situation. By the way, were the six examples given above *problems* or *opportunities*?

Tool 6: The Art of Problem Finding

At the heart of any client-oriented change process is the ability of your clients to find out what is preventing them to get from where they are to where they want to be. As the consultant, your challenge is to get them from where they are to where they want to be. We call this the art of problem finding.

Unfortunately, it isn't always as simple as it sounds. Finding the "real" problem can be complicated for several reasons.

Unclear goals. The client may not know where she wants to be in the future. Without a clear picture of what things will be like when the problem has been solved, there is no way to know if resources spent in problem solving are worthwhile. In other words, if your client doesn't know where she wants to go with the organization, for example, it may be difficult for her to know when she gets there.

Misreading symptoms as the problem. It is not unusual to mistake a problem for either a *symptom* or a *solution*. Both can mask the true nature of the problem and prevent the best of efforts to solve it. Symptoms are manifestations of a problem. They are useful in describing the problem. But focusing energy on solving a symptom without dealing with what is causing it will likely result in the problem coming back again. A familiar example is taking an aspirin to cure a headache (a symptom) but doing nothing about the conditions causing the headache (the problem).

Misreading solutions as the problem. Solutions can also masquerade as problems. The same person with the headache might define his problem as needing an aspirin. The aspirin is not the problem; it's a solution and possibly only one of many. The headache might be caused by noxious fumes coming from a leaky pipe.

Sometimes it helps to hold a dialogue with the problem. In other words, talk to it. Here are some questions the consultant and client can ask when confronted with something that looks like a problem.

- *What is the problem, the real problem?* This is a good starting point for separating problems from symptoms or solutions.

- *Why is it a problem?* This is a search for cause. The approach is to ask the question, get an answer, and then continue asking the question again each time an answer is given to the previous question. It's like peeling an onion to get to the answer that lies far beneath the surface. Although it sounds simplistic, the methodology is fool proof.

- *Why should the problem be solved?* If there is no good answer to the question, the problem, whatever it is, may not be worth solving.

- *When and where is it a problem?* This question can fix the problem in time and space and maybe provide some clues about dealing with it.

- *Whose problem is it?* Finding out who is affected by a problem can produce allies in finding a cause.

- *What really is the problem, and why?* Periodically returning to this fundamental question helps to find something useful that might have been overlooked the first time around.

- *What would happen if we didn't solve the problem?* There are situations where waiting out a problem will give it time to go away on its own. Sometimes, the best solution is to do nothing.

These questions will trigger a flow of information that can reveal the complexity of the problem and begin to suggest alternatives for solving it.

Tool 7: Engaging in Skillful Dialogues

Peter Senge and his numerous colleagues have done all consultants an enormous favor by exploring the fringes of how to bring about various kinds of planned changes through a wide range of interventions. *The Fifth Discipline Fieldbook* is rich in consulting-type tools and we encourage you to add this to your bookshelf and consulting bag. Since we just got finished talking about how you can help your client find "the problem," let's look at what Rick Ross, a Peter Senge colleague, has to say about situations where there seems to be no clear answer.

You, as a consultant, and your client often will be faced with complex and interdependent situations where no one individual can be expected to have "the answer." To cope with this complexity, you and your client—even though you all are informed and committed individuals—need a discussion process that encourages the parties to openly share and challenge each other's thinking: *"This is what I think we should do, and this is how I arrived at this conclusion. How does it sound to you? Can you see any way to improve on it?"* This method of first laying out an issue with the reasoning behind it, and then encouraging others to challenge it as well as offer their own ideas, is called "skillful discussion."

Rick Ross has developed five techniques that can help consultants and their clients engage in effective problem solving and decision making discussions.

1. *Pay attention to your intentions.* Individuals who are joining for a discussion will accomplish far more if they are absolutely clear from the start what they intend to accomplish by meeting. It is important for each person to be clear about what he or she wants from the experience and not to mislead others regarding these intentions.

2. *Balance advocacy with inquiry. Advocacy* is expressing your position and the reasoning behind it. *Inquiry* is encouraging others to challenge your position and offer their own ideas. These essential tools of skillful discussion have particular value when a discussion has bogged down and ideas and information from everyone in the group are needed to get things moving again. Here are some specifics on the process. Make use of advocacy as a discussion tool by:

   • stating the assumptions behind your position and describing how you arrived at your position using data, information, and other concrete information;

   • explaining the assumptions underlying your position;

   • being more explicit about how you arrived at this point of view

   • elaborating your point of view by explaining who will be affected, how they will be affected, and why;

   • providing concrete examples, if possible, and hypothetical ones if you are operating in new territory; and

   • trying to imagine the perspective of others about what you are saying.

Test conclusions and assumptions by:

- encouraging others to explore your ideas, assumptions, and data;

- not being defensive when your ideas are being questioned;

- indicating where you are least clear in your thinking about the position you are advocating and asking for their input; and

- listening actively, remaining open, and encouraging others to put forth their views.

Balance advocacy with inquiry by:

- helping others explore their own reasoning on the topic;

- explaining why you are interested in their points of view;

- testing what they are saying by asking open-ended questions;

- checking to see if you really understand what they are saying; and

- listening for comprehension to move everyone to a higher level of understanding and appreciation of each other's points of view.

3. *Strive for shared meaning*. Words are abstractions. They can have different meanings to different people. In most discussions, the conversation moves at such a fast pace that no one questions whether the words used actually mean what they were intended to mean. People can walk away from a discussion with a variety of distorted meanings and misunderstandings about what is to be done and by whom. Because this happens so often, it is important to use language with great precision in discussions, taking care to clarify the meaning of key words being used. Here is an example of how even the simplest word or phrase can be *misinterpreted*.

"You said 'Get it done.' But what is 'done'?"
"Well, 'done' means finish the report."
"Oh, so you're not including printing."

"I hadn't intended to. What leads you to think our definition of 'done' should include printing?"

4. *Use self-awareness as a resource.* Take a moment, when feeling angry, frustrated,or confused during a discussion, to pause and question what's going on inside you: *"What am I thinking? What am I feeling? What do I want at this moment?"* You may discover some insights about the assumptions others are making, or your own concerns, that you can bring out without blaming anyone: *"What you are saying implies an assumption about citizen involvement..."* or *"I am feeling uneasy about the direction we are going, and I'm not sure why."*

5. *Explore impasses.* Disagreements are more difficult to resolve when the source is unknown. Sources of disagreement fall into four categories:

   Facts: What exactly has happened?
   Methods: How should we do this?
   Goals: Where are we headed?
   Values: Why do you think this must be done in a particular way?

Agreement on the source of a disagreement is a big step toward getting it resolved. Ask yourself: What do we agree on? What do we disagree about? Can we pinpoint the source of the impasse? (1994, pp. 385-9)

The tools that we have just been discussing tend to be more interpersonal, ones you can use to be more effective in your interventions with others who are your client or who represent the client if, for example, the client is the organization or the community. We realize this is a bit of an intellectual stretch in defining the break between the tools we have just discussed and the tools that we will now present, but bear with us. After all, it's an imperfect world out there. If you haven't figured that out yet, maybe you should consider switching professions. Becoming a mortician where some things tend to be finite may be a better job for you.

Tool 8: Strategic Planning As an Intervention Strategy

Within the major category of organization development and institution building intervention strategies is the process of strategic planning. And, within strategic planning are a number of tools that can be used for other purposes. *Stakeholder analysis*, for example, is useful in almost every problem solving situation. Yet it often is associated as an integral step in the strategic planning process. This point is made not to add confusion but rather to avoid it. Unfortunately, it is one of the dilemmas in allowing others, like you, to mess around in our toolkit.

Management and consulting literature is filled with descriptions of methods that leaders, consultants, and organizations employ when engaged in forward planning. Visioning, stakeholder analysis, SWOT (if you haven't been swot-ed yet, we will take care of that injustice in a few moments), and action planning in its infinite variations are future-oriented methods of intervention that come to mind immediately. The dilemma that makes our lives untidy in arranging these tools for placement in your toolkit is the ambiguity that surrounds them. While they can be used independent of one another to achieve a particular organizational change objective, they more often are employed as part of a more extensive, integrated, step-by-step approach called *strategic planning*. Given this conundrum, we will paint the big picture and then break out some of the various tools so you can use them in an array of consulting situations.

John Bryson, a recognized authority on the subject and, incidentally, an intern in Fred's office when he was a city manager back in the last millennium, describes strategic planning thusly.

Strategic planning is a comprehensive, participatory and stakeholder driven effort to produce decisions about the identity, purpose and work of an organization that shape and guide its future actions. (1988, p. 5)

When undertaken effectively, strategic planning involves honest self-analysis, extensive information gathering both inside and outside the organization, a thorough exploration of alternatives, orderly decision making, and the assignment of responsibility for implementation. Its strength as a formal planning tool can also be a weakness. When strategic planners become preoccupied with procedure and detail, they can lose sight of the "big picture."

Strategic planning often begins when someone, i.e., a local elected official on her own initiative, or on the suggestion of a senior manager in the mayor's office, or even at the urging of some outside influence group, gets agreement of key others to launch a strategic planning effort. This initial decision would best be followed by these actions:

- Of course, the client should engage the services of a consultant like you, who has the credentials and experience in conducting such strategic planning meetings.

- Together, you and your client for this intervention would determine what individuals, groups, or organizations, i.e., stakeholders, should be involved in the planning effort.

Although opinions differ on how to undertake the strategic planning process, one dominant school of thought is to follow an approach that takes those involved through a series of sequential step-by-step activities. The following is a description of these steps.

- **Step One**: *Stakeholder identification and analysis.* Identify those persons, groups, or organizations that can place a "claim" on the organization's attention, resources, or outputs and which should be involved in the planning process, or, at a minimum, satisfied by its accomplishments.

- **Step Two**: *Mission clarification.* Clarify the reason why an organization exists, based on how well it meets the social, economic, and political needs of its stakeholders.

- **Step Three**: *Environmental* scanning. Examine factors outside the organization's control (*opportunities* and *threats*) and factors inside the organization (*strengths* and *weaknesses*), such as what the organization does (performance); how it does it (processes); and with what resources (staff, finances, material, etc.). If you put the first letters of each of these factors together in the right order, they spell SWOT.

- **Step Four**: *Issue identification.* From results of the preceding step, identify strategic issues facing the organization, framing them as questions to be answered later in the planning process.

- **Step Five**: *Strategy* formulation. Formulate broad courses of action designed to manage or overcome the issues that affect the organization's mission and impede progress toward its vision.

- **Step Six**: *Visioning*. Develop an ideal view of the organization or the environment of which the organization is a part (i.e., the community or region).

Note: The process of strategic planning can encompass many analytical and decision-making tools that can also stand alone and be used to address other client-centered needs. For purposes of describing how these tools can be used to facilitate the strategic planning process, the next six tools will follow the six steps outlined above.

Tool 9: Identifying and Analyzing Stakeholders

Generally speaking, stakeholders are any person, group, or organization that is affected by either the causes of an issue or the consequences resulting from it. For example, air pollution might be caused by persons in the community who are burning trash, while those affected from the consequences might include children with respiratory problems.

For the purposes of strategic planning, stakeholders are individuals, groups, or organizations that have an interest in the rationale for, or outcome of, the planning process. While stakeholders most often are selected because of their advocacy and what they can do to support the process, those who might be opposed to either the planning process or what it might produce should not be ignored. Their inclusion in the process could be an important way to neutralize their opposition or possibly convert it into support. In addition, they often bring a different perspective to the discussions which can be invaluable to a planning group that has been engulfed by its own enthusiasm for developing a strategic plan for their organization or community.

Assuming the organization wanting to conduct the planning process is a local government, stakeholders would probably include key members or all of the governing body; public managers and technicians who would be responsible for implementing the strategic plan; representatives of the business community; key civic organization leaders; and leaders of community-based constituents. In other words, stakeholders are those who have an interest in the planning process and its outcomes.

Conducting a stakeholders' analysis should be a simple process. Reaching final agreement on what stakeholders will be involved in the strategic planning process may be another matter. Identifying and analyzing stakeholders involves several steps.

Step One. Identify the stakeholders who for the reasons already mentioned should be represented in the planning process. Have participants at an organizational meeting individually prepare stakeholder maps (see *Figure 1*). The results later could be consolidated for discussion by the planning group. This individual approach gets everyone's ideas about who the stakeholders should be to the planning process. Consolidating the lists will quickly determine who are the most frequently mentioned stakeholders.

Step Two. Prepare a list of each stakeholder identified in Step One and help those involved to answer two questions regarding each of the proposed stakeholders:

- Why should this stakeholder be involved in the strategic planning process?

- What is needed or wanted from this stakeholder?

Step Three. Narrow the list of potential stakeholders to a reasonable number, based on the information gathered from Step Two. In order to do this, it might be helpful to establish criteria for selecting these individuals or the organizations or groups they represent and then to put priorities on both the criteria and those who make the initial selection list. Recognize that this may be a politically sensitive process.

If some of the stakeholders that have been identified are either groups of individuals or organizations, it might be important for the selection of their representative(s) to be the prerogative of the group or organization. It's important to increase their commitment to, and ownership of, the process. Inviting them to make the final selection of who will represent their group or organization can be an important step toward these goals.

Figure 1: Stakeholder (bubble) Map

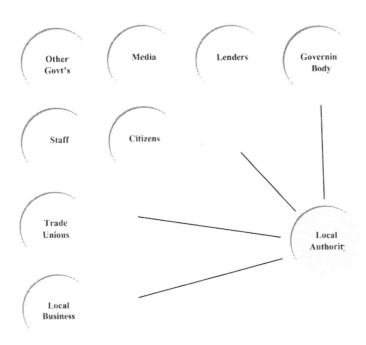

Tool 10: Developing Mission Statements

A mission statement describes *why* an organization should be doing what it does. An effective mission statement usually has two distinct roles and responsibilities:

- Whatever is included in the mission statement should conform to the law, the organization's charter, and other generally accepted standards of performance for an organization of this kind.

- Mission statements should also reflect desirable social, economic, cultural, and political goals that bring focus to the rest of the strategic planning process and create enthusiasm and commitment among members of the organization.

Members of a strategic planning group, including representatives of stakeholder groups identified in the preceding step, should be asked to answer several questions that will help them better determine the elements of a mission statement. It will be helpful to provide the planning members with a worksheet containing these questions along with blank spaces for answers. Please note that the questions are written as though each member of the planning team is an integral part of the organization for which they are writing the mission statement—hence such queries as,

1. *Who are we?* Helps to draw a distinction between what the organization *is* and what it *does.*

2. *In general, what are the basic social, economic, and political* **needs** *or the social, economic, and political* **problems** *we as an organization are expected to address?* Helps to visualize the organization as a means to an end and not an end in itself.

3. *In general, what do we want to do in order to recognize or anticipate and respond to these needs or problems?* Helps participants attend to real problems and needs outside the organization to stimulate innovative thinking.

4. *How should we respond to our key stakeholders?* Helps to clarify the kinds of relationships the organization wants with its key stakeholders.

5. *What is our philosophy and what are our core values?* Helps to keep strategies that will come out of the planning process remain consistent with what really matters to the organization's members.

6. *What makes us distinctive or unique?* Helps to keep the focus on what the organization does that no one else can do as well, if at all. (Bryson, p. 105)

While each member of the planning group should contribute his or her ideas via this written assignment, the actual task of writing a mission statement should be turned over to a single individual. This task should not be delegated until after a thorough discussion of each individual's contributions and a group consensus has been reached about the important elements to include in the mission statement. The resulting draft then can be discussed and any amendments agreed upon and adopted. The finished documents should be printed in large type and placed in a prominent place so as to be visible to the planning group throughout the process.

Tool 11: The Environmental Scan (SWOT Analysis)

Strategic planning is a data-driven activity. It is concerned with finding the best possible fit between an organization and its environment based on what is already known about the organization plus what is learned from an assessment of internal (strengths and weaknesses) and external (opportunities and threats) factors. Many of those with whom you work will probably recognize these four factors as the elements in the well-known SWOT analysis technique. The strategies that eventually emerge from the planning process are effective only to the extent that they take advantage of the organization's strengths and opportunities while minimizing its weaknesses and threats.

A simple technique called "snowballing" is a productive way to carry out an environmental scan based on SWOT analysis. Snowballing consists of five steps.

Step One: Participants, seated at a table (or tables of about five to nine persons), are asked to write down as many answers as possible to this question: *"What major external opportunities do we see?"*

Step Two: Participants are asked to select from their individual lists the five "best" ideas for answering the question and to write each of the selected ideas legibly on separate index cards.

Step Three: Participants are asked to tape their cards to the wall and then, as a group, to select thematic clusters for use in re-grouping the cards with an identifying label for each cluster.

Step Four: To conclude, participants are asked to discuss, compare, and contrast the results.

Step Five: At the session's end, the cards are collected in order and typed onto a spreadsheet for distribution to participants. (Nutt and Backoff, pp. 257-8).

The environmental scan continues, using the same idea generation/synthesizing process to compile three more lists initiated by these questions:

- What major external threats do we face?

- What are our major internal strengths?

- What are our major internal weaknesses?

This process will generate an impressive data bank of ideas and information from which to continue the strategic planning process.

Tool 12: Strategic Issue Identification

Identifying strategic issues is at the heart of the strategic planning process. The purpose of issue identification is to identify the fundamental policy choices facing the organization. (Bryson, p. 139) It is at this point in the process when many participants begin to realize that strategic planning is not an academic exercise. Strategic planning, as a direction-finding and defining process, has real consequences for the organization and its constituents when adopted as public policy.

Strategic issues should jump out of the SWOT analysis conducted in Step Three. They normally come in several varieties, mirroring the internal strengths and weaknesses as well as the external opportunities and threats just identified. For example, strategic issues might arise:

- when events beyond the control of the organization (threats) could make it difficult for the organization to achieve program purposes within existing resources;

- when human, technical, or political factors associated with achieving the organization's purposes are, or soon will be, changing, thus posing either threats to or opportunities for the organization;

- when internal or external events might provide opportunities to improve service quality and cut costs by merging certain services and eliminating others.

The process for identifying strategic issues begins by asking participants to complete a thorough review of the results produced by the environmental scan after which participants are asked to answer these three questions:

- *What is the issue?* Be sure to phrase the issue as a question about which the organization is able to take some sort of action.

- *Why is it an issue?* What is it about the organization's mission and the lists of external opportunities and threats, and internal strengths and weaknesses, which make this an issue?

- *What are the consequences of doing nothing about this issue?*

Composing strategic issue statements takes time for review, thought, and reflection. Bryson and others suggest that participants be given up to a week to compose their answers. When scheduled to meet again, participants are asked to write each of their issue statements on large sheets of chart paper that can be posted on a wall for review and discussion by other participants. This time span, which encourages reflective thinking on the part of all planning participants, may not be realistic in many cases. If not, other approaches should be considered. For example, many organizations consider this process so important to the future of their organization that they arrange for the participants to meet off-site, or out of the community, for a 3-4 day residential work session.

Back to the issue identification process. Consider grouping the issue statements using a thematic cluster approach similar to the one used to process ideas from the environmental scan. This can be useful to facilitate a decision by participants on a final list of issues.

Tool 13: Formulating Management Strategies

Strategy is the bridge between the current reality of an organization and a desired future state. It is a planned approach involving a combination of policies, programs, activities, and resource allocations to overcome obstacles and take advantage of opportunities for the achievement of organizational purposes.

Some authorities distinguish types of strategies that might result from a process of strategic planning. Each is based on different organizational expectations. (Nutt and Backoff, pp. 289-90)

- *Quality strategies* are positions or actions an organization might take to improve service performance or lower the cost of a service.

- *Acceptance strategies* lead to the adoption of policies or programs that would be held in high regard by governing bodies or other prominent stakeholder groups if adopted.

- *Innovative strategies* consist of policies or plans derived from previously untested ideas that might result in new ways of doing things.

- *Preservation strategies* are policies or positions designed to protect policies, programs, and work relationships that are not to be challenged or changed.

Based on the SWOT analysis and the issues identification process, the planning team, assisted by the consultant, is ready to develop a set of strategies. Bryson recommends the following five steps to formulate the strategic plans management strategies.

1. What are the practical alternatives that we might pursue to address the issue?

2. What barriers do we anticipate to the realization of these alternatives?

3. What major proposals might we consider to achieve these alternatives directly or else indirectly by overcoming barriers to their realization?

4. What must be done within the next twelve months, using existing staff and other resources, to implement the major proposals?

5. What specific steps must be taken within the next ninety days to implement the proposals and who is responsible for getting this done? (1995, p.139)

Some organizations and communities may find it effective to ask the planning team to answer the first two questions based on the SWOT analysis. The task of developing answers to the other three questions might then be delegated to special planning task forces, committees, or individuals. The answers would be brought back to the planning team for review and a final decision. The strategic plan gets very specific at this point in the process. Otherwise, it is, more often than not, headed for the top shelf in some important person's office where it will gather dust.

Tool 14: Visioning

The final step in the strategic planning process is to establish a clear and compelling picture of what the organization will look like after strategies have been successfully implemented and the organization is achieving its full potential. This step is placed at the end of the process rather than the beginning to guide and encourage strategy implementation.

Vision has been defined as "an ideal and unique image of the future." An inspirational vision:

- Focuses on a better future.

- Encourages hopes and dreams.

- Appeals to common values.

- States positive outcomes.

- Emphasize the strength of a unified group.

- Uses word pictures, images, and metaphors.

- Communicates enthusiasm and kindles excitement. (Krouse and Posner,1987, pp. 109-13)

Statements that embody the vision of an organization should be short—not more than a couple of pages, well articulated, and inspirational. A useful way to begin constructing a vision statement is to have strategic planning team members reconvene to answer two questions:

1. What will our organization (community) look like five years from today if we fail to implement these strategies and continue to function as we have in the past?

2. What will our organization (community) look like five years from today if we succeed in implementing these strategies and are uniquely and dramatically transformed by them?

These highly contrasted questions are meant to result in alternative scenarios about the organization's future that are distinctly different. The first scenario clearly conveys to those involved the tragic consequences of inaction. The process to be used proceeds as follows:

Step One: Using an idea generation technique, preferably the Nominal Group Technique (NGT), the planning team develops a list of answers to the first question. The most realistic and insightful results are selected by the group and posted by the consultant on a sheet of chart paper.

Step Two: A list of answers to the second question is developed in the same manner.

Step Three: A member of the team with a gift for composition or some-one with similar skills from outside the team is asked to draft a one-page vision statement by a specified date for review by the team.

Step Four: Team members meet to review the statement and make a decision about its adoption, revision, or re-drafting. As a guide to deci-sion making, the consultant might suggest the following set of criteria and scales to rate the statement's acceptability. (Nanus, 1992, p. 219)

Criteria	Rating Scale 5 = highest; 1 = lowest				
Future oriented?	1	2	3	4	5
Appropriate?	1	2	3	4	5
Reflects high ideals?	1	2	3	4	5
Clarifies purpose?	1	2	3	4	5
Inspires enthusiasm?	1	2	3	4	5
Reflects uniqueness?	1	2	3	4	5
Realistically ambitious?	1	2	3	4	5

When general agreement is reached on the style and wording of the vision statement, arrangements should be made to circulate it among members of the organization and external stakeholders.

The final set of tools we want to share is more inclined to be used when you are helping a client bring about large systems changes in, for example, organizations or communities. Like the tools asso-ciated with strategic planning, we will introduce you to a big tool box containing some all-purpose tools that have broad use in the consulting business. The mega-tool box we are talking about is action research. Descriptions of the individual tools that have broad application in this business appear after our discussion of action research.

Tool 15: Action Research: An All-Purpose Larger Systems Change Strategy

Kurt Lewin, one of the first acknowledged behavioral scientists, made numerous contributions to what we now think of as the consulting profession. Among the most important was something he called *action research*, a collaborative approach to systematic decision making and problem solving which is at the heart of just about everything the process consultant does. He was known to his colleagues as the "practical theorist." Through a series of steps, which are not always sequential, the consultant guides the client, be it a group, organization, institution, or community, to design data gathering processes and plan system-wide changes based on the analysis of the data.

While it sounds very complicated, action research has some built-in learning factors that help just about any social system to accomplish its goals through this collaborative and self-correcting process. Here are the most important characteristics of action research as a consulting tool.

- *Action research (AR) is a conceptual framework for thinking about problems as well as a managerial philosophy that can be used to center all activities.* In Lewin's terms, "No action without research; and no research without action."

- *Action research involves widespread consultation and participation.* Everyone involved in the problem is seen as capable of making a contribution. AR is based on the fundamental belief that people are more likely to change if they participate in exploring the reasons for, and the means of, bringing about change.

- *Action research puts a premium on learning by doing.* Learning, and consequently training, is built into the heart of the process. The intent is not simply to solve immediate problems, but to help those involved in solving current problems gain the knowledge and skills needed to solve future problems.

- *Action research is practical and direct.* It is carried out within the context of real issues and concerns defined by those involved.

- *Action research is developmental.* It causes individuals, teams, and organizations to become more self-reliant.

- *Action research is experimental.* It encourages experimentation and practice in addition to recognizing the importance of using that which is learned to guide that which is yet to be done.

- *Action research is sensitive to the cultural context of its involvement.* While the process of action research may not be totally free of cultural biases, it can and should be responsive to cultural differences, given its built-in feedback and self-correcting features. Don't be put off by the cultural reference. Organizations, communities, and even groups develop cultural traits.

Think of action research as the overall conceptual framework within which we can manage group, organization, and community changes; a set of principles and values that encompasses the change process; and the strategy that drives each of the eight tactics we are about to describe for your enlightenment and use.

Action Research Is a *Strategic* Process Involving Eight *Tactical* Steps

In other words, action research is a collaborative process consultants can use with confidence to help various kinds of clients manage social, economic, technical, and other types of changes within their organizations and communities. This strategic process is composed of eight tactical steps.

1. **Awareness and Vision.** Awareness is the ability to see problems as they are; vision is perceiving opportunities that don't yet exist. Both are invaluable skills in helping clients bring about change. Applying awareness to problems and vision to opportunities are also when we think, "Who else should I involve—can I involve—in helping solve this problem, realize this vision?" In other words, work with your client to do a *stakeholder analysis.* As Chiu Ming said many centuries ago, "The way of war is to know your opponents." We will put a more positive spin on this proverb by saying, "The way to manage change is to know your stakeholders."

2. **Building a Problem Solving Relationship.** Like the foundation of a house, the relationship of the people engaged in problem-solving is the base upon which all future actions rest. When that relationship is one of mutual trust and understanding, the

process of making decisions and solving problems is greatly improved. Building the relationship means:

- Sharing expectations and values.

- Setting ground rules.

- Assuming useful roles and responsibilities.

- Learning how to work as a team.

3. **Problem Finding and Analysis.** Deciding what problem to solve or what opportunity to realize is not as easy as one would think. Sometimes it is necessary to *redefine* the problem or opportunity, even if your client has decided what it is. It is not uncommon for managers to identify symptoms as problems (which they often are) but the *problem* with "solving a symptom" is that the real problem still will exist. Or, managers define a solution as the problem and this, of course, eliminates all other options as potential solutions to the problem. After helping your client to determine what the *real problem or opportunity is,* the task of analyzing it becomes much easier. Nevertheless, analysis involves a number of critical skills.

   - **Planning a Course of Action.** Having identified the real problem (or opportunity) and analyzed it, the next step is to decide how best to plan for its implementation. This involves:

   - Narrowing your choices to one priority action.

   - Looking at the potential consequences (what will be the impact, short term and long range).

   - Developing a plan of action (to implement the best action, or a combination of actions).

Choices are the manager's best friend. Without choices, it is impossible to *manage.* No choices, no need to decide. If there is no need to decide, who needs a manager? Planning a course of action is deciding *who will do what with whom within what time frame. In addition, you must identify the necessary resources and determine how you will know your plan was successful.* Planning involves making decisions. It's an important management responsibility and therefore shouldn't be left solely to planners.

5. **Organization and Resource Mobilization.** In most client systems, the organization and its employees are the biggest single, on-going, most immediately available resources. How they are organized and deployed to accomplish any organizational change strategy is important. Equally as important are all the other resources: money, expertise, equipment, materials, time, commitment, goodwill, "power" connections (those with sufficient clout to help your client clear an important unexpected hurdle), and, yes, customers or citizens, depending on whether your client is a private or public institution.

6. **Experimentation, Testing, and Redesigning.** Too many promising solutions are "implemented" without a field test, controlled experiment, or trial run. Before you help commit your client to dive into deep water with a major untested organizational change endeavor, it makes sense to try out any proposed plan in "the shallow end of the pool." This allows the problem solving team to assess how effective and workable its proposed plan of action will be, and to redesign it if necessary.

7. **Implementation.** This is where clients put plans into action. Implementation also involves managing the intended and unintended consequences of the rigorous planning process. Even if the plan of action you helped your client develop is well thought out, anything can happen. Consequently, it is important to have backup plans. And one backup plan is to have your client retain your services to track the implementation progress or, in some cases, lack of progress.

8. **Impact Evaluation.** This involves helping the client get answers to such questions as: *Did we do what we intended to do? If not, why not? Did the change have the intended impact (outcome) we anticipated? If not, why not?* As a consultant, you can perform a valuable role for your client in tracking the progress on systems and decisions that you have helped put into place.

Anyone can break something up into small pieces.
The trick is to knit them back together again into
a whole without compromising their autonomy.

David Nadler

Action research is both a theory about the conditions needed to bring about organization or system changes as well as a process for applying the theory to solve real problems experienced by a client organization. The consultant who approaches problems from the perspective of action research not only aids the client to solve a specific problem but leaves the client far better prepared to deal effectively with future problems.

Strategic planning and other long-range and intermediate direction finding ventures, which often use action research as the operational strategy, require a data and information base. In this final set of tools, we will look at various ways to generate decision-making information and data bases.

Some General Thoughts on Developing Information and Data

As a consultant, you may be asked to intervene in the affairs of organizations when something goes wrong. The client may have correctly diagnosed the problem and now is seeking help to find the right remedy. Or, the client only knows that things are not working as they should and wants help to find out why before exploring what to do about it. In just about every situation where a consultant is engaged to help a client, there will be an immediate need for more information and data to better understand what's behind the problem or to validate possible remedies. Whether the information needed has to do with work processes, equipment design, employee attitudes, or some other aspect of the client's operation, there are several choices to be made by the client and consultant. For example, they need to:

1. *Identify the surface problem.* Using a version of the *problem finding* method described earlier in the manual, the purpose of this early step is to find out more specifically what is bothering the client. The intent is to verify or redefine the problem as well as unmask symptoms and solutions that may be disguised as the "real" problem.

2. *Agree to proceed.* On the basis of what is learned from problem finding, the consultant and client agree to proceed, assuming there is a mutual desire to commit time and resources to a study that has promise for organizational improvement.

3. *Set limits.* This involves deciding on the questions to be asked and the areas of the organization that will be involved in the data gathering effort. Limiting the questions is important to keep the volume of data gathered from becoming overwhelming. Questions can be asked of people inside the organization (employees, managers, elected leaders) or outside (citizens, customers, representatives of other stakeholder groups). They can be asked questions about facts, behaviors, or attitudes. Keep in mind that asking people questions will raise their expectations about receiving feedback on the information they have supplied.

4. *Select data collection method(s).* How the data will be collected is based on the size of the study, the motivation of the managers concerned, and the nature of the problem to be solved. Data can be collected by interviewing, either face-to-face or by telephone; surveying by pen and pencil questionnaire, telephone, or computer; document review; and direct observation.

5. *Collect the data.* Implement the data collection method or methods selected.

The following are the most frequently used techniques for gathering data and information.

Tool 16: The Interview Technique

The interview is a method of data collecting in which the questions and responses are given orally and usually face-to-face. The most important characteristic of an interview is that the interviewer can ask additional questions to those included in the original interview plan. This can be useful if the response from a person being interviewed is not clear or complete and a second set of *probing* (follow up) questions might produce a more satisfactory response. More specifically, the interview is a good choice when:

- The object of the inquiry is not well known and changes might be necessary during the course of the interview;

- The range of response can't be predicted and the respondent may present information or viewpoints that are new and unexpected;

- The questions being asked are related to the unique personal views and special insight of the respondent;

- The cost in time and travel to conduct interviews is affordable;

- Some respondents may have trouble expressing themselves in writing.

Interviews can be time-consuming. Given the frequent need to travel to and from the interview site, not more than three or four can be completed in a day, including the time required to document the results of the interviews. This may require the consultant to limit the number of interviews or to get help from others trained in interviewing skills.

The value of an interview can be diminished by extraneous factors that can *bias* (distort the accuracy or truth) the respondent's answers. The potential for bias can be reduced by choosing surroundings familiar to the interview respondent that are as free of distractions and interruptions as possible. The interviewer can help by never expressing her own opinions about the topics being discussed.

Interviews are begun with a statement about their purpose, how the results will be used, and the degree to which the respondent's answers will be kept confidential. Normally, interviews proceed from general questions to more specific ones. Questions are "open ended" (see the earlier material on discussions), and probe questions are used as needed to encourage the respondent to explain or amplify responses. Sometimes probes are used to bring focus to what the interviewer wants to know, e.g., *Can you tell me more about that? Why do you think that happened?* Other probes are used when it is suspected that the respondent may have overstated an answer and might want to reconsider, e.g., *Are you saying that...? Do you really mean that...?* Such probes would then be followed by a rephrasing of the answer.

Documenting interview results can be complex and sometimes frustrating. Notes are sometimes incomplete or unreadable. Even tape recording can be problematic, and tapes may have to be listened to several times to fully grasp the meaning. If the interview is to be taped, it is important to get agreement from the person being interviewed.

Despite best efforts to avoid it, bias can creep into an interview. If the interview has produced what appear to be important factual statements, a couple of unfortunate possibilities should be considered. The respondent may have embellished or misconstrued the facts; or, the respondent may be limited to only one side of a story.

Tool 17: The Survey Questionnaire

The survey questionnaire is a popular and convenient way to get answers from multiple respondents to straightforward questions. Respondents may live far away from the person conducting the survey and even far away from one another. The questionnaire can be filled out and returned in the mail, as an attachment to an e-mail message, or to a designated person within the organization requesting the survey. The survey questionnaire is a good choice when:

- The problem for which the survey is being conducted is well defined and will not change during the project;

- The questions to be answered are known in advance and the survey is meant to discover only how the range of answers is distributed within the survey population;

- The questions involve facts, quantities of things, or polarized responses like "yes" or "no";

- There are questions included in the survey that respondents would only answer anonymously;

- The results are meant to be easily subjected to some form of quantitative analysis.

Survey questions are about matters of fact or opinion. A fact question might ask for a person's year of birth or to check a block indicating marital status: *single, married, divorced, widowed*. Such questions must include the full range of possibilities or else provide an extra box labeled *other*. Questions about facts must be absolutely unambiguous (free of double negatives or obscure words) since the respondent has no way to ask for clarification. To avoid the possibility of confusion or misinterpretation, *pre-testing of survey questionnaires is essential*.

Another common problem with surveys is that respondents are not always truthful. They may answer questions in a way that would give a more positive picture of their income, education, or other circumstances related to their social status. When this is suspected or likely, a confirmation check of the survey sample with official records could detect these discrepancies. Or, the questionnaire might be designed to ask similar questions in different ways in order to spot inconsistencies.

When the questions being asked are about opinions or attitudes, certain steps should be taken in questionnaire design.

- Make use of statements that are provocative in order to create respondent interest.

- Avoid questions with obviously right or wrong answers.

- Keep the sentences short and simple.

- Avoid words like *all, always, no one,* and *never.*

Scales are often used in questionnaire design to allow respondents to choose the degree of their reactions to survey questions. Examples are levels of agreement (a five point scale with a range from *totally agree* to *totally disagree*) or degrees of importance (a five point scale with a range from *very important* to *very unimportant*). The collective results can be transformed into mathematical frequencies and analyzed statistically (arithmetic averages, frequency distributions, correlations, etc.).

Tool 18: Document Review

The history of any client's organization is preserved in its own official records and in official information compiled by others about the organization. Access to this information can provide the consultant with valuable insights about why and how the organization does what it does. The time it takes to learn about an organization can be a valuable source of clues about the organization's problems and enables the consultant to speak more intelligently about them with organizational insiders. Document reviews have two distinct advantages over other data collection methods: They can be performed by a single person without the need for advanced planning or special forms, and since information is collected from documents rather than people, the usual issues related to obtaining information from people are avoided.

A manual on training needs assessment published in the early nineteen nineties by UNCHS-Habitat illustrates the wide range of subjects about which a consultant might seek information from written records.

- Evidence of *organizational purposes and directions* that might include policy statements, budget documents, annual reports, minutes of governing body meetings, laws and regulations, program descriptions, and quotes from speeches.

- Information on the *human resource* side of the organization, including the organization chart, employee turnover and vacancy rates, new job openings, internal capacity to fill vacancies, and requirements for outside recruitment.

- Evidence of organizational performance, including documents like budget status reports, service complaints, accident/injury reports, equipment repair and out-of-service records, and project status reports.

- Evidence of *employee satisfaction or dissatisfaction* that might include disciplinary reports, service or performance rewards, promotions, service complaints, employee grievances, and absenteeism. (1992, pp. 28-32)

Document review is rarely the only method employed by a consultant. It is normally supplemented by the results of conversations and direct observation. Document review can equip a consultant with important background and an insider's understanding about events and circumstances related to the problem the consultant has been asked to solve. A consultant who has taken time to review important documents can often speak with more authority and assurance about the organization and the circumstances involving the consultancy.

Tool 19: Direct Observation

Observation is a visual method for gathering data about an event, a process, or someone's behavior so the results can be recorded and used for later analysis. The consultant who gathers data by direct observation, e.g., watching as a project team meets to work on a task, goes directly to the source, thereby avoiding the problem of distortion inherent in obtaining information secondhand from others through interviews or surveying. While direct observation is no more important than other forms of data collection, there may be circumstances when it is the only reliable way to gain insights about what is going on.

Direct observation might be useful when conflicting reports from parties representing the two sides of a labor-management dispute prevent a consultant from understanding the real cause of difficulty. The answer may come from direct, personal observation during a meeting of the parties. This form of observation may give the consultant the proof she needs to state with conviction that what has been said during a conversation or even learned from a survey is valid in explaining what is causing a problem or what should be done to resolve it.

Direct observation may be the data collection of choice for a consultant when it has been scheduled or prearranged to facilitate the orderly assembly of data about some aspect of organizational performance; it has been triggered by a request from the client; or some chance event provides an opportunity for this direct data-gathering approach. (1992, pp. 34-5)

The following is a more in-depth look at these data-gathering opportunities.

1. *Scheduled observations.* Prearranged observations allow a consultant to be present at times and places when problem-related activities may be taking place. The intent of the observation is to verify the conditions that contribute to the problem under study and to remove from consideration those which have nothing to do with it. A consultant attempting to explain a productivity problem in a department, for example, might watch as similar work is done in other departments to determine factors that might account for the performance variations.

2. *Triggered observations.* Sometimes consultants are invited to be present for an event that the client has concluded is a problem. The consultant's task is to verify that the client's assumption is correct and, if so, what might be done to remedy the situation. For example, a consultant might be asked to attend a bimonthly meeting of a local governing council and to suggest what might be done to shorten the council's excessively long meetings.

3. *Chance observations.* Opportunities arise from time to time for a consultant to spot a discrepancy in performance although she is not specifically looking for it. Such observations might have direct, indirect, or no bearing on the problem under study. The consultant, for example, might be seeking information from a client's file only to discover that the filing system in use is badly organized and contains large volumes of dated and superfluous material. Depending on the nature of the relationship with

the client, the consultant might point out the consequences of poor record maintenance and offer suggestions for corrective action to the appropriate supervisor.

Observation methods are subject to observer bias. The manner in which the consultant conducts the observation or her very presence can cause those being observed to behave differently than they would when the consultant is not present. Reducing this form of bias is important. Consultants should try to be as unobtrusive as possible during observation sessions. It is helpful for a consultant to arrive early at the location of the meeting or other event to give those present a chance to overcome their initial curiosity and settle down before the event being observed begins.

> Earlier we mentioned the tool that Kurt Lewin created in the early days of behavioral science approaches for resolving complex social, economic, and organizational problems. Well, here it is!

Tool: 20 Force-Field Analysis

A well-known method in every consultant's toolkit is *force-field analysis*. This analytical technique was first proposed by Kurt Lewin in the late 1940s as a way to better understand social problems and plan corrective actions. It is based on the assumption that the current state of affairs in an organization, or in the behavior of an individual for that matter, is the way it is because opposing forces work to maintain a state of equilibrium. A different state of affairs can be achieved, according to Lewin's assumption, by unbalancing the forces that are preventing change. In other words, to move things from the current state to the desired state requires the addition of forces favoring the change or removing forces that oppose it. The technique has application to any kind of social problem: rising crime rates, declining productivity, group morale, joblessness, etc. Force-field analysis involves the following six steps:

1. *Status quo.* An assembled group is presented with the problem to which a solution is to be found. Participants are asked to discuss the problem. What is the current situation? Why do you want it changed? The problem, for example, might be *uncooperative behavior of customer service clerks responsible for the issuance*

of construction permits. The behavior is creating ill will with customers and delay in the permit granting process. Ideas are recorded by the consultant on a chart pad.

2. *Future state.* Participants are asked to define the conditions they hope will exist when the problem is solved. How would you define correct behavior? The desired condition related to the preceding example might be described as *fast, efficient, and courteous response to customers requesting permits.* Ideas are recorded by the consultant on a chart pad.

3. *Identify the forces.* Participants now are asked to identify the forces that are pushing conditions in the direction of the desired change and the forces that are maintaining conditions where they are (forces that oppose efforts to do things that would eliminate or lessen the problem). The consultant should urge participants to exhaust the possibilities on both sides of the equation. An example of the kinds of forces favoring and opposing a change in the behavior of counter clerks is shown below in the diagram.

4. *Analysis.* Participants are asked to examine the forces. Which forces are strong and which are not so strong? Which are susceptible to influence and which are not? Which are under the client's control and which are not? Key ideas from the discussion can be recorded on the chart pad.

5. *Strategies.* Ideas for moving the equilibrium from the current situation to the desired future state are considered. They might involve adding more driving forces, removing restraining forces, or both. Lewin cautions against simply adding more driving forces since this can cause more resistance. The better approach is to develop strategies for the removal of the most important restraining forces.

6. *Action plans.* As time permits, participants can be asked to develop action plans that would add new driving force strategies or, more preferably, remove or weaken restraining forces.

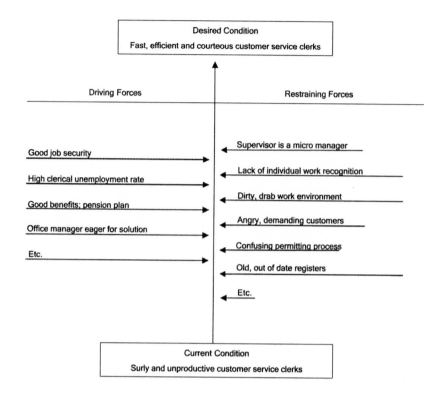

Tool 21: Training As a Consulting Service

We close our tool kit by looking at one of the best tools you have for not only being successful as a consultant but cloning yourself as a consummate problem fixer and capacity builder. When you are successful in providing various kinds of services to an organization, you no doubt will be requested to follow-up with some type of management or staff training. This is particularly true when you are engaged in *process consulting* and the client sees the potential for her staff to become more proficient in various kinds of interpersonal, planning, and decision-making skills. Or, you may be involved in helping to install a new human resource management system on personnel evaluation. A logical follow-up would be to train those who will be responsible for implementing the new system. Since mastering the full range of training knowledge and skill areas would involve a whole new guide, the intent here is to provide only an overview of the training cycle and the types of tasks involved in carrying it out.

The training cycle begins when a training need is found (input) that calls for a training response (activity) that produces a learning result (output) that eventually leads to a redefinition of needs for learning and growth. The training need may involve individuals; groups of individuals, such as a team; or an entire organization. This concept of training as a continuing response to the learning needs of the intended audience is shown in the diagram below.

THE TRAINING CYCLE

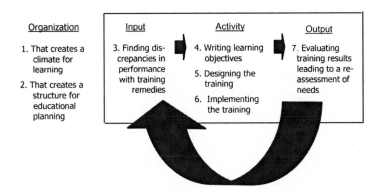

The input side of training. A performance discrepancy is the difference between what management expects from an employee, team, or department, and what they actually are producing. The discrepancy could be caused by a lack of knowledge or skills, which could be addressed through a training intervention. Or, it might be caused by some other variable, i.e., lack of proper equipment. The consultant will need to do a training-needs assessment (TNA) to determine why the performance discrepancy(s) exists. This is where those data and information tools, discussed earlier in the Guide, will come in handy.

Your TNA, conducted through interviews, surveys, document review, and observations, should produce a lot of information regarding the performance discrepancy under investigation. Typically, this information also will include much that is non-training related. You will need to sort out the performance discrepancies you can address through training and feed the rest of the information back to the manager for consideration. Since you wear both the training and consulting hats in this venture, you are also in a position to help the client address the non-training specific needs. Once you are confident about what the training needs are, you can move into the activity phase of the training cycle.

The activity side of training. There are three considerations on the activity side of training:

- *What is to be achieved by the training?* Learning objectives are necessary for planning a training program and determining after the training is done whether or not it has been a worthwhile investment. Without preparing clearly stated objectives in advance, neither of these essential components of training is likely to be done to anyone's satisfaction.

- *What approach to training design is most appropriate?* Several approaches can be considered for achieving training objectives. One is to send those to be trained to an open-enrollment program designed and conducted by an outside training institution. Another is to employ a training consultant to come in to conduct the training based on the organization's objectives and specifications. A third is to train members of the organization's staff to conduct the training. Which approach is best depends on the number of people to be trained, the technical complexity of the training, the quality, suitability, and cost of outside training, and the availability and skills of staff to do the necessary design work and implement the training plan. While all alternatives are appropriate, the latter two offer the consultant an opportunity to continue the client-consultant relationship. On the other hand, the consultant should not take on a training assignment he is unequipped to carry out to the satisfaction of the client.

- *Doing the training.* There are several important considerations in implementing a training design. First is *entry*: Warm up and get acquainted activities are essential to break the ice and ready people for exposing themselves to new learning experiences. Second is *sequence*: Give people something new to think about (short presentation), involve them in reflecting on it and contrasting it with their own experience (group discussion, case study, etc.), and give them a way to evaluate its merits for use in their own work environment (individual skill development or small group application exercise). Third is *dynamics*: Deliver concepts and ideas in short bursts and allow participants time to process them thoroughly before moving into new material. Finally is *coverage*: It is better to cover a few important things thoroughly than rush to get through a lesson plan that was unrealistic in the first place.

The output side of training. Evaluation is management's strategy for calculating training's impact on and contribution to job and organizational performance. Evaluation can be used to determine increasing levels of training outputs and outcomes: participant satisfaction of the training experience (post training reaction sheets); determination of how much learning has taken place (instrument results and testing); and specific changes in the behavior of trained individuals and the impact of this behavior on the organization and its environment (supervisory assessments, cost/benefit analysis, customer satisfaction surveys). Returning to the diagram, evaluation can lead to the discovery of previously unrecognized needs and establish the basis for more or different kinds of training or changes in work processes that are not knowledge or skill related.

Providing training services for your clients adds a whole new dimension to your consulting business. Much of what you do as a consultant involves potential learning opportunities for your client. By expanding your consulting skills to include training, you offer your clients a value-added dimension to your services. In order to expand in that direction, you may need special training as a trainer. That, of course, goes beyond the scope of this Guide. After all, we need to hold back on our infinite knowledge about this business, just in case this tome sells.

VII. Time to Set Yourself on Fire

Fred was walking down the street in Kampala, Uganda many, many years ago when he saw a sign in front of a little fruit stand being operated by the oldest, most withered-up, bent-over-with-age lady he had ever seen. It read:

**STOP BEING
IDLE HERE
PLEASE!**

She was so busy sweeping the fallen leaves and trash away from her modest business establishment that she nearly knocked him over as he walked by. She was an entrepreneur on a mission. On the other hand, she may have been a down-on-her-luck consultant just putting in time until *Successful Consulting* was written and published.

Now that you have read *Successful Consulting* and completed all those assessment instruments and worksheets, it's time to offer you a bit of African advice: **Stop being idle here, PLEASE!** But before you rush out the door, let's go over some of the key points we think are important to be even more successful than you currently are as a wannabe or struggling consultant.

Go back and revisit the self assessment questionnaires in the opening chapter, the *Moment of Truth* Inquiries. We can never be too sure about who we are and what we want to do in the consulting business. And while you're at it, sit down with your significant other, or your best friend, maybe your financial advisor, and do the *Financial Reality* Challenge in the second chapter. Prices keep going up on everything, in case you haven't noticed, and you may be headed for a big *billable day* migraine down the road. If you don't feel justified in raising your professional fees at this time, look at the many options we have outlined that will help you satisfy your current and long-range financial needs and yearnings.

Unless current and future clients are beating down your door, we hope you found some good advice in Chapter III about marketing your services and further developing your business. Put it to use and maybe they will beat your door down. In case this happens, keep the authors of *Successful Consulting* in mind. We never turn down referral business.

William Shakespeare, a bard of some renown, said, *Give every man thine ear, but few thy voice.* It's rather strange advice for a consultant, who must rely heavily on the mouth for a living, but nevertheless an important bit of sagely wisdom from a person who freelanced for a living. Even the most successful consultants stop from time to time to reflect on how they are communicating. Why? Because Richard Barham, in his 19th c. ballad *Misadventures at Margate*, describes the consultant's worst nightmare. *When the Town Crier cried, 'O yes!' the people cried 'O No!'* Before this happens to you, check out all the great communicating skills we suggest in Chapter IV. You might even have a second career as a bard or balladeer.

Of course, the client relationship challenge we talk about in Chapter V is also important. If your career evolves like those of most consultants, you will be challenged to find new clients, or find yourself moving in new directions. A quick review of this chapter can help you define your future success—before it becomes a challenge.

Don't forget the twenty-one tools we provide in Chapter VI. Put them in your briefcase before you head out the door for your next consulting assignment. We have found all of them to be useful in our careers as consultants. The important thing is to keep adding to the tool kit, keep the consulting challenge alive, and remember the old German proverb, *when one is helping another, both are strong.*

Finally we want to remind you of something we said earlier in *Successful Consulting.* Success as a consultant is not the result of spontaneous combustion. You must set yourself on fire and continue to fan the flames if you want to be successful.

More about the Authors

Fred Fisher is a specialist in public management with an emphasis on capacity and institution building initiatives involving local governments, non-governmental and community-based organizations in developing and transitional countries. His more than forty years of professional service has been roughly divided between being a hands-on manager-and helping others learn and apply management knowledge and skills in a variety of public and third sector environments.

He is currently Director of the International Development Institute for Organization and Management (IDIOM). Prior to becoming a full-time consultant, Fred served as a regional housing and urban development specialist in eastern and southern Africa for USAID, taught at a major university for seven years, was the Vice President of the National Training and Development Service for State and Local Governments in Washington, and the city manager in Grove City and State College, Pennsylvania. Fred has master degrees from the Universities of Pennsylvania and Southern California and a doctorate from the University of Southern California. He has authored or co-authored more than fifty training and management manuals for UN HABITAT and other institutions.

Peggy Fisher started her career as a registered nurse and after taking the proverbial parental break to rear the family, returned to the workforce. Peggy's second career includes stints as the finance manager and executive vice president of a national education association serving the hospitality industry, property manager for a large diplomatic mission in Nairobi, Kenya, and co-director/finance officer for IDIOM.

Selected Bibliography

Biech, Elaine. *The Consultant's Quick Start Guide*. San Francisco: Jossey-Bass/Pfeiffer, 2001.

Block, Peter. *Flawless Consulting*. San Diego, CA: University Associates, 1981.

Bryson, John. *Strategic Planning for Public and Nonprofit Organizations*. San Francisco: Jossey-Bass, 1988.

Chrislip, David and Carl Larson. *Collaborative Leadership*. San Francisco: Jossey-Bass, 1994.

Cope, Mick. *The Seven Cs of Consulting*. (2nd ed.) London: FT Prentice-Hall, 2003.

Kouzes, James and Barry Posner. *The Leadership Challenge*. San Francisco: Jossey-Bass, 1987.

LeBoeuf, Michael. *Getting Results*. New York: Berkley Books, 1989.

Lewin, Kurt. *Field Theory in Social Science: Selected Theoretical Papers*. Ed. Dorwin Cartwright. New York: Harper & Row, 1951.

McLagan, Patricia and Peter Krembs. *On-The-Level: Performance Communication that Works*. San Francisco, CA: Berrett-Koehler Publishers, 1995.

Nanus, Bert. *Visionary Leadership*. San Francisco: Jossey-Bass, 1992.

Nelson, Bob and Peter Economy. *Consulting for Dummies*. New York: John Wiley, 1997.

Nutt, Paul and Robert Backoff. *Strategic Management of Public and Third Sector Organizations*. San Francisco: Jossey-Bass, 1992.

Putman, Anthony. *Getting Started in Consulting*. New York: John Wiley and Sons, 1990.

Senge, Peter, Charlotte Roberts, Richard B. Ross, Bryan Smith and Art Kleiner. *The Fifth Discipline Fieldbook*. New York: Doubleday, 1994.

Weiss, Alan. *Getting Started in Consulting*. New York: John Wiley and Sons, 2000.

Manual for Training Needs Assessment in Human Settlements Organizations. Nairobi: UNCHS-Habitat, 1992.

Index

G

Getting Results (LeBoeuf), 92

Getting Started in Consulting (Weiss), 83–84

goals and objectives
   of client, 100
   of consultant, 43

H

hidden costs, of self-employment, 30–31

honesty, 84, 85

I

income. *See* revenue

indirect marketing strategies, 50–51. *See also* direct marketing strategies
   examples of, 78–79

information and data collection, 6. *See also* survey and assessment techniques
   direct observation, 126–128
   document reviews, 125–126
   feedback from data, 71
   initial tasks in, 121–122
   interview technique, 122–124

Ingham, Harry, and Johari Window, 54–55

innovative strategies, 113

inquiry, as discussion tool, 103

intellectual properties, 84

internal consultants, 11

International Development Institute for Organization and Management (IDIOM), 137

interpersonal communication skills. *See* communication

intervention, 74
   definition of, 10
   types of, 90–91

interview technique, of information collection, 122–124

issue identification, 106, 112–113

978-0-595-36479-4
0-595-36479-9

Printed in the United States
59789LVS00005B/417